The Decadence of Industrial Democracies

For Barbara

The Decadence of Industrial Democracies

Disbelief and Discredit, Volume 1

Bernard Stiegler

Translated by Daniel Ross
and Suzanne Arnold

polity

First published in French as *Mécréance et Discrédit, tome 1: La décadence des démocraties industrielles* © Éditions Galilée, 2004

This English edition © Polity Press, 2011

Polity Press
65 Bridge Street
Cambridge CB2 1UR, UK

Polity Press
350 Main Street
Malden, MA 02148, USA

*CB
78
.S8513
20 11
v.1*

ISBN-13: 978-0-7456-4809-5
ISBN-13: 978-0-7456-4810-1(pb)

A catalogue record for this book is available from the British Library.

Typeset in 11 on 13 pt Sabon
by Toppan Best-set Premedia Limited

Printed and bound in Great Britain by MPG Books Group Limited, Bodmin, Cornwall

The publisher has used its best endeavours to ensure that the URLs for external websites referred to in this book are correct and active at the time of going to press. However, the publisher has no responsibility for the websites and can make no guarantee that a site will remain live or that the content is or will remain appropriate.

Every effort has been made to trace all copyright holders, but if any have been inadvertently overlooked the publisher will be pleased to include any necessary credits in any subsequent reprint or edition.

For further information on Polity, visit our website: www.politybooks.com

Contents

They have admired things that are hardly ever admired now, have seen truths living that are now nearly dead, have in fact speculated on values whose decline or collapse is as clear, as manifest, and as ruinous to their hopes and beliefs as the decline or collapse of the securities and currencies which they, and everyone else, once thought were unshakeable values.

They have witnessed the ruin of their former faith in spirit, a faith that was the foundation and, in a way, the postulate of their life.

They had faith in spirit, but what spirit? . . . what did they mean by this word?

. . . a world transformed by spirit [*esprit*] no longer presents to the mind [*esprit*] the same perspectives and directions as before; it poses entirely new problems and countless enigmas.

Paul Valéry[1]

My wound existed before me; I was born to incarnate it.

Joë Bousquet[2]

1

Decadence
And the Obligations it Creates for Us

All these values, rising and falling, constitute the great stock market of human affairs. Among them, the unfortunate value of *spirit* has not ceased to fall.

Paul Valéry[1]

There are those who find peace only through carelessness [*incurie*] in relation to all things.

Jacques Benigne Bossuet[2]

1. The political decadence of democracies is a crisis of the industrial model

At the time of the first genuinely European election in History, on 13 June 2004, there was a sudden aggravation of the political decadence that we, the French, had initially and then daily endured as a national reality since 21 April 2002, although we knew that it was eating away at other industrial democracies too. This same aggravation brought the ordeal to its true level: to the point where we must become capable of thinking of something other than limits [*frontières*], and of gathering our forces [*battre la campagne*] in order to project ourselves into the invention of a new process – that of a *supranational psychic and collective individuation.*[3]

We know from experience – and we were painfully reminded of this in 1992, the year Sarajevo was martyred, a city that had already become tragically historic on 28 June 1914, that point of departure that eventually led Valéry to write *The Crisis of Spirit*, in which he declared the mortality of civilization. Some years later, Husserl published *The Crisis of European Sciences*, in which he called for a large-scale *return to the question* of Europe, to the history and geography of the knowledge woven within it, which, since 1914, had become lost[4] – we know then, in advance, that Europe is also the level at which one can expect the worst, at the very moment when one believes it possible to seek out the best. Concerning borders [*frontières*], in Europe, we tell ourselves that anything could happen, as if the suppression of barriers from one side must be paid for by the raising of walls on the other side. With its past, full of spirit but haunted by phantoms, with its historical and geographical indefiniteness, and the incomparable quality of life of this '*petit cap*', of this sweet land that, as a patchwork of '*petites différences*', on occasion secretes such bitterness, could Europe yet again become a Pandora's Box?

Without wishing to be precipitously overdramatic, I pose this question because it brings us back to our common responsibility to ourselves, as Europeans, whoever we may be – at the moment when one feels that this possibility of the worst has become the only possible horizon of something better. Europe is a chance, and first of all a chance to avoid the worst, the worst that it could still become, in these times of historical precipitation, of extreme uncertainty, and of generalized changeability. One could say, as I did myself, that what took place in France on 21 April was a catastrophe – even if it was only, after all, a kind of quantification and, in some way, objectification of political decadence that certainly did not wait for this election to manifest itself, and which finds its sources in the hidden vices of democracy. Since it was the outcome of a vote and not an opinion poll, however, this quantification did have *performative* value. And to this extent it also constituted what might be called an *historic date*: if it is true that this electoral result contained nothing unexpected (it was foreshadowed in the municipal elections of 1983, and in the European elections of 1984), the success of the extreme right in the second round of the French presidential elections was an historic fact, where democracy encountered the limit revealing its *extreme weakness*.

I still believe that this encounter with History was a catastrophe, but my understanding of this word must be clarified (and I'll come back to this in the next volume of *La technique et le temps*, and in *De la misère symbolique 2. La catastrophe du sensible*). As a general rule, one calls *catastrophic* an event engendering chain reactions overturning a state of things that until then was close to an equilibrium stabilizing an order. A catastrophe is also, however, and first of all, a *strophe*: the *catastrophe* is the final episode of a history, the moment of a denouement. Now, this is a matter of human History itself (in this case, that of the women and men of France), and not one of those stories through which men and women talk about themselves, and recount and imagine a common history. Consequently, after this catastrophe, insofar as it is a *cata-strophe*, and if this is always in fact a matter of a catastrophe or, more precisely, of a moment inscribed within a catastrophic *process*, which we must understand as a process through which *one* history exhausts itself by *undoing* itself, French and European human History must nevertheless continue – as a History of France, or as some other History, which would pass through France, from out of France, but also, perhaps, from elsewhere, and from out of elsewhere. The *cata-strophe* must be the end of *a* history that would nevertheless have been a morsel of History, and *takes place* at the beginning of *another* history, connected to it in a way that is *more or less painful*, and *pursuing* History by inscribing within it a *bifurcation*.

The question then becomes to know, first of all, of *which* history this *catastrophe* would be the denouement.

It is in order to respond to this question, and to the question of the *possibility*, and the *necessity*, of connecting to – that is, *beginning – another history*, that in this work I attempt to describe some facts of a catastrophic nature, of which 21 April would be only one salient performative moment, and which are themselves inscribed in a context of generalized decadence, a decadence which is not only French, nor even European, but certainly global and, especially, *industrial*. Beyond all the talk, whether well-informed or naïve, illuminating or, on the contrary, intended to produce smokescreens, most of the time juridical,[5] *today's question remains the fact that an industrial model of production and consumption*

*has failed, and this question henceforth becomes a matter of reso-
lutely elaborating a critique.*

Such a critique (that must call on the resources of what I have
elsewhere called a *new critique*, in the sense of a philosophical
leap, an exit from the dogmatic slumbers that have accumulated
in the twentieth century in philosophy, but also in science) would
not be a denunciation: it must be an analysis of the limits of the
object of critique, and the *elaboration of a renewed idea of this
object.*

The necessity of such a critique imposes itself at a *crucial* stage
– at a crossroads where irreversible decisions have to be taken.
This failure appears at the moment, and even as the moment,
when the industrial model has become that of a *structurally cultural* capitalism. And this transformation, of which the United
States of America would be the crucible, leads, in the context of
upheavals [*bouleversements*] induced by digital technologies, to
that epoch of modern democracy that I have characterized as
hyper-industrial.[6]

2. The American construction of cultural capitalism and European servility

It is in the first place a matter of giving a critique of the *classical*
industrial model that was elaborated in North America long before
the hyper-industrial capitalist epoch. And yet, and principally to
overcome what Marx called its 'contradictions', this classical
model soon places *cultural control* at the heart of the process
through which it pursues its development. This has not been generally understood by twentieth-century analysts of capitalism
(with the possible exception of Gramsci and certainly of Adorno),
and it has been made especially unthinkable, after 1968, by
the sociological fable of the 'leisure society', also called 'post-
industrial society'.

In the United States, culture became a strategic function of
industrial activity from the beginning of the twentieth century. On
the basis of analogue recording and transmission technologies, a
new kind of industry was conceived, called the 'culture industry';
between the two wars, with radio, and especially after the Second
World War, this evolved into the 'programme' industries (in par-

ticular, in the form of television) functionally dedicated to marketing and publicity – contrary to European television, which has a function that is firstly political; in France, privatization, which seems today to be self-evident, only occurred at the initiative of François Mitterrand, who expected thereby to provide himself, cheaply, with a 'modern' image.

With the advent of very advanced control technologies emerging from digitalization, and converging in a *computational* system of globally integrated production and consumption, new cultural, editing and programming industries then appeared. What is new is that they are technologically linked by universal digital equivalence (the binary system) to telecommunications systems and to computers, and, through this, directly articulated with logistical and production systems (barcodes and credit cards enabling the tracing of products and consumers), all of which constitutes the hyper-industrial epoch strictly speaking, dominated by the categorization of hyper-segmented 'targets' ('surgically' precise marketing organizing consumption) and by functioning in real time (production), through lean production [*flux tendus*] and *just in time* (logistics).

In this context of the upheavals induced by digitalization, often compared to a 'third industrial revolution' (also called the 'information society' or, more recently, the 'knowledge society' – the digital system permitting, on the side of industrial conception, the systematic mobilization of all knowledge in the service of innovation) – a process unleashed by the adoption of the TCP-IP standard, that is, through the creation by the USA of a worldwide digital network called the Internet – the rest of the 'northern countries' adapt themselves poorly or well to the 'American model': the industrial democracies ape it more or less poorly, and submit themselves to its prescriptions, repeating like a flock of parrots the ideologemes which these organs of propaganda diffuse over the planet as so many *deceptions and lures* [*leurres*]. The principal of these consists in claiming that public power is obsolete and in decline, and in *performatively creating political decadence*, while never ceasing to appeal (up to a certain point) to human rights and international law to legitimate the political poverty [*misère*] of nations. This movement is produced in the wake of the 'conservative revolution' ushered in by Ronald Reagan at the beginning of the 1980s (preceded by Margaret Thatcher in Great Britain in 1979, and followed by Tony Blair).

Now, at the same time, not doing what it says it will do, and not saying (to those who still credulously submit to the recommendations of what continues to be called 'governance') what it does, the American federal government invests massive public funds in the development of these cultural technologies: billions of public dollars have been invested for twenty years in information technology. American public power thus guides – and with remarkable lucidity – the global strategy of American power, in constant cooperation with the business world, but in the end imposing its vision upon it. In spite of this, the other industrial countries, reputedly democratic, under the leadership in Europe of the European Commission, apply without any critical distance alleged 'best practices', practices consisting in the liquidation of all thought and all public will, by abandoning all decisions about the future to 'market forces' – except when it is a matter of applying the dogma of 'perfect competition',[7] that is, the *total* execution of market laws. So-called democracies slowly but surely lose their specificity, that is, also, their legitimacy and their credit, as well as the forces constituting their historical and cultural singularity.

Because in what way is it still a matter of '*democracy*'? What is a demo-*cracy* that can no longer decide its *kratos*? And if it is true that democracy is the power of a *demos*, then it remains to be shown that a juxtaposition of *consumer* niches still constitutes a *demos*. In fact, the *demos* is a *process of adoption*, as is, in its turn, but differently, 'consumer society'. To understand in what way consumption is a rupture in the relation to citizenship depends, firstly, on understanding what is pursued through these profoundly different forms of social organization: a process of adoption.

In the sixth century BCE, Cleisthenes – after Solon had, around 594 BCE, written the law and *constituted the* demos *in law* – created the *demes* in order to break down the tribes and the clans of archaic Greece (in 508 BCE): the members of these *demes*, who may be foreigners or even slaves, henceforth took on the name of their *deme* while adopting the prytanic calendar.[8] This was a matter of alleviating the burden upon cities constituted by socio-ethnic programmes (in Leroi-Gourhan's sense, on which I commented in *Technics and Time, 2: Disorientation*[9]), and which still haunts what Dodds called the 'Inherited Conglomerate',[10] that is, those traditional elements maintained within the new Greek culture, which is a political culture – that is, from Solon to Pericles and via Cleisthenes, democratic culture.

As such an adoptive process, the *demos* tries to resolve questions, questions which then find themselves replayed in industrial societies, insofar as these societies find it constantly necessary to adopt new arrivals in order to fulfil their need for unskilled manual labour, but also and above all insofar as these societies require the adoption of *new products*. The *demos* is a *regulated adoption through a law that is* itself *public*, that is, elaborated politically, such that it poses in principle a difference between right and fact. This model is maintained in spite of all the transformations characterizing the history of the Western European process of individuation, up until the end of the nineteenth century. Today, however, the adoptive process implemented by the United States no longer remains democratic in this sense: it is *consumerist*.

3. Adoption, technology and public power in America

It is in the context of the passage to the hyper-industrial and *structurally cultural* era of capitalism, on the way to effective globalization, where consumerism (completely replacing the *social* control in which all culture consists with a *behavioural* control conforming instead to the interests of investors) tends to efface the democratic character of what one continues to call the 'industrial democracies' (referring today more to 'human rights' than to the *citizenship* inaugurated by Cleisthenes) – it is in this context that the American government developed the strategy that was portrayed by David Rothkopf in the following way:

> For the United States, foreign policy must be to win the battle of the world's information flows, dominating the airwaves as Great Britain once ruled the seas.[11]

This 'battle of the flows' aims to supply new models, consisting of technologies of digital behavioural control made possible by the convergence of information, telecommunication and audiovisual technologies. What is being gestured towards with such American declarations (in particular, those advanced by Al Gore and Bill Clinton concerning the 'information superhighway') is the same thing that in Europe is called the 'information society', and this is what engenders all the mirages of the 'new economy'.

The 'battle of the flows' rests on global public access to the Internet network, but also on the replacement of the analogico-hertzien audiovisual technical system. This replacement was announced by the American government on 3 April 1997, when the FCC[12] indicated that the closure of the analogue frequency television broadcast band for US territory would occur in 2006,[13] to be replaced by a new *totally digital* audiovisual technical system, already being installed, and very far from having unfurled all of its effects, which will be immense. By conjugating the access to digital telecommunication networks made possible by the TCP-IP standard, on the one hand, with the digitalization of audiovisual transmission enabling the digital compression of image and sound through the MPEG standard, on the other hand – or, in other words, by organizing at a global level the convergence of telecommunications, the audiovisual and information – the United States is orchestrating, at its own rhythm and according to its own interests, an immense technical mutation which spells the end, for the West, of more than a century of analogue information technologies and communications technologies. The global mnemo-technical system – which, as will be shown in the next chapter, constitutes *a new stage of the grammatization process lying at the origin of the West*, and which has overdetermined the individuation process in which the West has consisted – has therefore today become the heart of a planetary technical and industrial system. This is a fact of which the European public powers are obviously still unaware, even though the spread of medium- and high-speed telecommunications, as for example with ADSL and broadband technology, has already transformed the disc industry, and will soon transform the entirety of what economists call the 'editorial function'. Beyond this, however, it is the totality of industrial activity – reorganized around globally connected digital networks and machines, and thereby *functionally integrating conception, production, distribution and consumption* – that is being profoundly altered. And I will show in the following pages that *one of the principal effects of this is that the cultural question becomes the heart of industrial policy* – an issue that has thus far been profoundly ignored by the European public powers.

This sovereign decision of the FCC is inscribed in the industrial and technical policies of the American federal government, which chose to privilege the digital long before the arrival of Bill Clinton (it is for this reason that the US constantly refused to participate in the discussions between Europe and Japan at the end of the 1980s about high-definition television standards), and which, far from leaving the 'invisible hand' of blind markets to their '*laissez faire*' work, instead conforms to the slogan of the Xerox Research Center, a slogan that one could say is typical of American culture and power in general:

The best way to predict the future is to invent it.

But in the United States, this invention is not merely an affair of the business world: it is a *public* strategy, animated and debated by a public *power*, which anticipates the future well beyond the short-term calculations made by markets.

Beyond the position of power held by the United States, the supremacy of the American programme industries – a supremacy that has been considerably accentuated and enlarged through the functional integration of digitalization in the passage to hyper-industrial social models – rests before anything else on the historic capacity of this country to *conjugate* a *politics of adoption* and a *technical politics*. As a migrant country, America has always had to elaborate a public policy of integrating immigrants, and, at the same time, it has always had to affirm the necessity of adopting the products of an industrial innovation that is constantly accelerating.

Adoption and innovation are the two categorical imperatives directly combined by American society and are the basis of its incomparable dynamism. Since the appearance of the industrial technologies of sound and image that made them possible, the culture industries have become organs capable of creating identification processes via behavioural models, behavioural models which are themselves incessantly renewed according to the demands of innovation. I have shown elsewhere (notably in *De la misère symbolique 1*) that the implementation of these *technologies of the sensible*, inaugurating what can be called the age of *industrial aesthetics strictly speaking*, also included a reflection on the consequences of the Freudian theory of libidinal economy for the economy as such, and, more generally, included 'research on motivations' enabling their artificial elicitation – it being understood that *the libidinal economy is the fundamental mechanism of all adoption.*

In other words, an industrial political economy must be a libidinal economy – the question being, however, to know to what degree this is not self-destructive, that is, to know the point up until which it not only preserves and guarantees but intensifies the existence of what Valéry called *spiritual economy*. I will return to this point in detail in what follows, and in particular in the second volume.

American federal public policy has therefore never been content – contrary to what continues to be repeated by European industrialists, politicians and bureaucrats – simply to 'follow the market'. The enormous American public and private investment into research and thought in all their forms (science, literature, art, philosophy) clearly constitutes the preliminary condition for that audacity which North America has consistently demonstrated. Beyond this, however, when in 1992, after careful consideration, America organized and permitted the access of all the countries of the entire world to the Internet network, this constituted the most glaring example of the *way* in which this country conceives the possibility of transforming its global environment according to its own vision: by thinking *simultaneously* about technological development *and* about the pursuit of the adoptive process in which *humanity in its totality* consists, and which then becomes a matter of taking planetary control.

4. The *motives* of European becoming and of the European *constitution*

Digitalization is a mutation of the global technical system – and globalization is before anything else globalization of the industrial technical system, 'democratic' or otherwise. Now, *each time a major technological rupture occurs*, it is imperative that this process be accompanied by governments, and other forms of public power, that want to take part in defining it. And such an accompaniment can in no way consist in a pure and simple *management* of that crisis which always results from a *disadjustment* between the mutating technical system and the other social systems without which it cannot function.[14] This process constitutes what I have called an *epokhal technological redoubling*,[15] that is, the suspension, by a technical or technological revolution, of a state of fact. Far from simply managing the effects of such a suspension, the public powers must on the contrary be capable of defining the *motives* conferring on the individuation process of the technical system its social and political meaning, that is, its *dynamism*, which presupposes its inscription in the psychic and collective individuation process in which human society consists, and which, as I return to at length, can only move, can only find the motives of this movement, on the condition of *cultivating singularities* that alone can constitute it as a process of psychic (and *psychically promising, that is, desirable and desiring*) individuation. This is what I call the redoubling of the *epokhé*, or, again, the doubly *epokhal* redoubling.

The evolution of the technical system forms the basis of the becoming of human societies and itself constitutes an individuation, in the sense defined by Simondon, and which I have developed further elsewhere. But the *becoming* [*devenir*] that this individuation constitutes is only possible on the condition that it is transformed into a *future* [*avenir*] by its insertion into *psychic and collective* individuation. This is what I argued in both *The Fault of Epimetheus* and *Disorientation*. It has sometimes been said to me, in particular after the publication of *Aimer, s'aimer, nous aimer. Du 11 septembre au 21 avril*,[16] that the tone of my writing has changed, that I have become 'pessimistic', and that I have, in the end, changed my understanding of the question of technics and technology. Now, I have always said that the becoming of the technical system requires, in order to *become the future* [*devenir l'avenir*] of the society in which it is produced, the *doubly epokhal redoubling*, which means that, within this complex process that is psycho-social individuation, the first *epokhé*, the first suspension of established order, is the *technical mutation* suspending a dominant state of fact, but equally means that society must also carry out a *second* suspension in order to constitute *an epoch properly speaking*, which means: in order to elaborate a *new thought* that translates into *new ways of life* [*nouveau modes de vie*], and, in other words, that affirms a new *will* for the future, establishing a new order – a civilization, a reinvented civility.

The present work is concerned with examining what prevents the accomplishing of this doubled redoubling as the *invention* of new ways of life. A thought only has meaning if it has the force of *reopening* the indetermination of a future. But it can only be a matter of new ways of life if those lives are constituted by *new modes of existence*: human life is an existence. Now, our current situation is characterized by the fact that this fails to occur, and that, in place of the necessary creation of these new modes of existence, there is substituted an *adaptive* process of *survival*, in which possibilities for existing disappear, being reduced instead to simple modalities of subsistence. This is what I have called *symbolic misery* [*misère symbolique*: symbolic misery, poverty, or immiseration – trans.]. Human beings can without doubt subsist without existing. I believe, however, that such a subsistence is not sustainable: it becomes, rapidly, psychically and socially unbearable, because it leads inexorably to the liquidation of primordial narcissism. And this liquidation in turn leads to the liquidation of the law. That is, to the liquidation of what constitutes the condition of a *demos*: a difference between fact and right. This is the meaning of the crime carried out by Richard Durn, assassin of the representatives of the French people – of the *demos*.[17]

Today Europe, and the industrial democracies generally, fail to operate this double redoubling, and *this* fact lies at the heart of the contemporary political and industrial question. Most political discourse avoids this fact – the manner of this avoidance stretches from the denial of the unavoidable reality of the first redoubling (conservatism, archaic environmentalism) to the denial of the necessity of the second (neoliberalism), and between the two lies a strange, stagnant marsh. As for the model installed in the United States, and which was the reason for its strength, this is now exhausted. It is for this reason the United States has been led into war, however much the accidental motives for this war may be tied to the apparently unbalanced psychological personalities of those such as George Bush and Osama bin Laden – and to which the history of their families is obscurely tied.[18]

One might object at this point that the chronic instability of technical becoming, which is characteristic of our epoch (this is what I have called *permanent innovation*), makes impossible the stabilization of an epoch, and thus that the redoubling is *structurally impossible*. I, however, completely disagree. But I do, on the other hand, believe that such an objection is grounded in real and unprecedented facts that must be taken into account with great care: it is necessary to rethink redoubling as requiring *an entirely new thought of what an epoch in fact is*, and in particular it must be thought precisely *as a process* rather than as a *stasis*, a process of individuation *putting individuation itself at the heart of its motives of action*, as the *principal motive*, constituting the motive *of its thought*, what I, after many others, call its *reason* – its reason to *be*, and its reason to *become*.

Redoubled or not, technological mutation is today pursued digitally, but also biotechnologically,[19] and, if nothing happens in the short term, then European democracies will soon be definitively enslaved, and the entire world disorientated [*déboussolé*]. Such is the true question of a European *constitution*, for which it is a matter less, today, of drafting a text – it is completely premature, given the current situation of immense indigence when it comes to political thought, to want to define what would amount to nothing more than mere vocabulary – than of inventing a new European process of individuation, emancipated from formal legalism and economism, by elaborating a programme of action projecting, through the clarity of its intrinsic necessity, its own *motives* of action.

Now, the first question to be posed in this regard is the complete absence of an original European policy in relation to the culture industries, and, beyond or within such a policy, in relation to artistic *research* and scientific *research*, whether in the human or in the natural sciences. While American paradigms dominate the majority of the university programmes of the entire world, a properly *European* artistic and cultural life, that is, borne, intended and sustained by European power, is practically non-existent. In its edition of 2–3 May 2004, the *New York Times* published a very ironic and incontestably just article, affirming in its title that 'A Common Culture (From the USA) Binds Europeans Ever Closer':

> As 10 new countries prepare to enter the European Union on May 1, it is not so much economic weight or political tradition that has earned them the right to join the regional bloc. Rather, it is a certain cultural identity forged by Christianity and a common artistic heritage. In one crucial sense, then, the lingua franca of this expanded Europe remains that of Shakespeare, Leonardo, Mozart and other giants of the past.
>
> Turn to the contemporary arts, however, and a different picture emerges. Here the union's old and new members alike know surprisingly little about one another's artistic inventiveness today. Creative life may be flourishing in widely different ways across Europe, but the most common cultural link across the region now is a devotion to American popular culture in the form of movies, television and music.[20]

The indigence of European political thought induces *negligence* [*incurie*] – this means *lack of care* and, as such, *carelessness*, *insouciance*[21] – in its actors, public or private, economic or political, academic or artistic, generally reinforced by the smallness of their interests, whether patrimonial or moral, corporate, disciplinary, economic or national, through all of which Europe is in the course of transforming itself into a gigantic museum. Hence, Paris: global capital of tourism. This museum might well be that of modern art, since this was born in Europe, and principally in France, in the nineteenth century – and thus it is already nearly 200 years old. And where this museification is not occurring, various 'zones' appear instead, territories abandoned by the spiritual economy in Valéry's sense, but over-invested by the hyper-industrial libidinal economy, that is, I argue, an economy that is self-destructive, and within which, precisely for this reason, resentments accumulate (I am speaking here about industrial and commercial zones, rural and 'technopolitan' development estates, etc.) – these zones amounting to something like the becoming-suburban of any region not 'patrimonialized',[22] Europe thus becomes a land

without ideas, without courage, and without future – because it
is without desire.

What has not been understood on this old continent is, on the
one hand, that the unity constituting a process of individuation is
first of all a singular cultural *sensibility*, and, on the other hand,
that this is not a matter of opposing industry to culture in order
to maintain this culture and this industry, as the nineteenth-
century romantics, then the moderns, constituted them. *Nor*, conversely, is it a matter of submitting all spiritual life to the
imperatives of the economy and technological development, and
to value spirit only in relation to these imperatives, as the neoliberal ideologues believe. Rather, and to the complete contrary, it is
a matter of the invention of a new order, and the constitution of
a *new model* of *industrial development* as well as of cultural *practices* (and practices *irreducible to mere usages*), at the very moment
that culture, or rather the *control* of culture, has become the heart
of development, but has done so at the cost of a becoming-herdish
which is also a generalized becoming-wild [*devenir-inculte*], and
which can only lead to political disbelief [*mécréance*, which could
also be translated as 'mis-belief', but also as 'miscreance', that is,
as bad behaviour – trans.] and discredit.

*It is a matter, in other words, of reconstructing a libidinal
economy* (a *philia*), without which no city, or democracy, or industrial economy, or spiritual economy, is possible.

5. Industrial policy must become a cultural
policy of technologies of spirit

In this respect, the policy that has been implemented in France
since 1981 merits particular analysis. If it is true that François
Mitterrand cheaply presented an image of modernity through his
audiovisual policy, then this was particularly true of the way that,
when he privatized part of the national television broadcaster –
creating Canal Plus, but also offering La Cinq to Silvio Berlusconi,
which fortunately turned out to be a fiasco – the president of the
French Republic nevertheless utterly dispensed with any rethinking or re-missioning of the audiovisual public service: he and his
technocratic apparatus *believed in neither the necessity nor the
possibility* of political action in this domain. It was for them

simply a matter of the *de facto* management of the slow and silent extinction of a model conceived by Charles de Gaulle and André Malraux.

This is how the *catastrophe* was brought about: the audiovisual domain is where opinion, the *demos*, and demagogy are constructed, and this is also the domain that is in the course of ruining what Paul Valéry called 'spirit value' [*valeur esprit*] – by spreading and generalizing the hyper-synchronization of consumer consciousnesses, which are thus formed into markets, so-called 'audiences', to the detriment of every other vocation. This much is clear: it was an initiative of the social democrats that enabled Patrick Le Lay to become the director of the main national television channel, even though that kind of 'dirty work' is normally carried out by right-wing governments. This non-belief of political power in the political power of public audiovisual missions, but also more generally in the *political responsibilities entailed by the appearance of technologies of mind and spirit*, in other words, *this cynicism*, the price of which is that political manipulation which consists in making political power amenable to the mass media, all in the name of modernity, in order to get elected or re-elected (as Tony Blair would do with Rupert Murdoch), this *political non-belief or miscreance* automatically engenders *discredit*, that is, also, and necessarily, violence, hatred, reactivity (in Nietzsche's sense), and the worst temptations.[23] This is far more serious than the mere 'loss of confidence' that 'observers' of our 'predicament' constantly comment upon. And yet, as I show in the next chapter, it is a certain understanding of confidence or trust [*confiance*] as an object of possible calculation that contributes to the liquidation of belief as the experience of the indeterminacy of the future [*avenir*], beyond becoming [*devenir*], the openness of a future irreducible to calculation, and that can only be the object of a *will*, that very will that has been renounced by the new unbelievers who are thereby discredited – and who are legion, far beyond politicians and their immediate servants. Now, trust does not exist without belief.[24] *Trust, calculated*, and reduced to this calculation, is thus automatically ruined: this is the *very principle of the decadence of the industrial democracies*.

And what Mitterrand – who so greatly wanted to become a great man, an historic figure, and a statesman, and who was himself also a great calculator, perhaps ultimately too great a calculator not to remain a little man – failed to understand was, on the one hand, that politics is above all the motivation and organization of a psychic and collective individuation process, and, on the other hand, that in our epoch this process is produced essentially via information and communication technologies, first of all via television, and, today, via the new culture industries, which are the vehicles of all symbolic exchanges, whether up close or at a distance. For anybody purporting to propose a politics, it is a matter of elaborating a critique of this process, in order to promote a new model, as well as to enunciate its structural limits, paralogisms and antinomies – that is, its duties, rights, obligations, prohibitions and *mysteries*.

Renouncing all ambition in this domain as in so many others, 'pragmatic' and brainwashed, socialist reformism – taking over from Valéry Giscard d'Estaing, who created a genuine rupture with Gaullist public power – installed a state consumerism that consisted not only in allying itself to the mass media, thereby alienating itself while also risking a mental alienation of society, but consisted as well in favouring mass distribution, always in the name of modernity, in order thereby to gain political benefit from the pressure exerted on producers to lower prices and flood the market with products 'as seen on TV', all of which ensures the distribution of bread and circuses, but destroys town centres, peripheries and suburbs, as well as social organizations and *psychic* organizations (self-image) – not to mention all those extra little benefits that come with what is called corruption.

Taken to the level of European questions, this political misery, which has also been the cause of a great economic misery, and which finds its alibis in the impossibility of ignoring the transformations of the surrounding world, fails to think through the meaning and the causes of these transformations, and ignores the fact that psychic and collective individuation is an adoptive process, the intelligence and robustness of which depends on the degree of its originality, and on the adhesive force that, as expression of a singularity, it gives rise to in the form of the desire to be together that Aristotle called *philia* – and it is not possible to understand why this desire must be renounced, other than because of the *weakness* of our *spirit*, that is, also, of our libidinal energy, of which spirit is nothing more than the sublime expression.

Now, weakness does not amount to fatality: it is a *resistible* fact. Because this spirit is the fruit of an economy: this economy is what must be made into the object of care, of a *cura*. This care is called *culture*. I will show in the course of this work that this culture is that of a *difference* between what the Romans called *otium* and *negotium* – and that this difference is not an *opposition* but a *composition*, and that for this reason economic models can be elaborated from it, even if these always and necessarily extend beyond any model and all economy, as with the economy of gift and counter-gift described by Marcel Mauss. And it is for this reason, equally, that the culture industries are not inevitably harmful, or worse – and it is for this same reason that, finally, they must *also in principle* be capable of the *best*.

Europe – which copies American economic models but fails to grasp that the cost of turning globalization into a generalized mimetism would be that it sinks into disaster – has resigned itself to delegating to the American entertainment and games industry the destiny of its own culture, that is, the *liquidation* of its own culture. Now, this is especially serious when, capitalism becoming cultural, culture itself becomes the key to all industrial policy – besides which, it was already the key to all politics whatsoever. It must be hoped that those European industrialists who are not blinded by ideology or paralysed by the voracity of their share-holders know how to preoccupy themselves, and be concerned with, posing the right questions, those which guarantee a *future* to industry – and where the much-touted reform of casual labour [*intermittence*] could only ever have amounted to rearranging the deckchairs in a situation in which everyone would nevertheless remain lost and deceived.

A European industrial politics of the future must understand technological development as an essentially cultural question, and must understand the cultural question from out of the question of *tekhné*, the Greek name for what we call art. A genuinely European industrial politics would require a complete rethinking of cultural politics in relation to everything that has been transformed by the industrial revolution and by the newest technologies, *but also* in relation to the *impasses* to which the American model has led, particularly in this domain. Without such a politics, there will be neither a European 'constitution' nor a European 'construction' worthy of the name: the process of adoption, which can only be effective as the expression of a *singularity that it invents to the degree that it draws itself together [rassemble]*, a process without which no European *affirmation* will ever take place, remaining instead essentially governed by American power, that is, it will not produce any singularity, but will on the contrary be reduced to a *regional particularity* which will become, from then on, and this time concretely, the American empire, supported by hyper-industrial technologies and by the cultural hyper-industries that they elaborate – until this in turn collapses.

Because this model will itself inevitably lead to its own collapse: stretched to its limits, it has become largely entropic and self-destructive, not to mention, equally and necessarily, hetero-destructive. More and more tempted into armed conflict, it must constantly increase police powers. Nobody would today believe that America is the 'land of freedom', and especially not since the Patriot Act came into force. This is a tragedy for America, the consequences of which it will have to suffer, but it is also and especially a tragedy for us, who follow this development like sheep, if not like lambs – but even so it is necessary, at this point, to salute the clairvoyance and courage of the foreign policy of the French government in relation to the conflict between Iraq and the United States.

6. The genesis of the American multimedia strategy

During the 1980s, American industry, which had by then surrendered a large portion of the market for consumer electronic equipment (to the increasing dominance of Japan and Europe), came to understand that reconquering this market passes through multimedia, that is, through the simultaneous digitalization of text, image and sound, and through the deployment of telecommunications networks totally transforming the way these are broadcast and communicated. Almost completely dominating the information industries, that is, computer technology, the United States created the conditions for a change which was largely based on the implementation of new industrial standards, in particular norms governing interoperability between networks (TCP-IP, which is the technical basis of the Internet), as well as norms for the digital compression of analogue signals (MPEG), that is, images and sounds, permitting *control to be taken of the entire field of cultural technologies*, that is, of editorial systems, audio-visual broadcast channels, networks and databases, and so on. Simon Nora and Alain Minc had by 1977 already foreseen this possibility, when they presented a report commissioned by President Giscard d'Estaing on the industrial stakes of the evolution of information and communications technology (ICT) – which, despite its break with Gaullism, the government nevertheless hoped to anticipate.

Today, throughout the expansion of the American multimedia industry, which drives the totality of global technological development and, with it, the rules and standards governing access technologies, as well as the standards governing what Jeremy Rifkin has called *relational technologies* (even when these standards have been conceived outside the United States: such is the adoptive capacity of this nation), it is a matter of controlling new culture industries, and their production of texts, images, sounds, hypertexts and hypermedias. The development of these technologies and industries, constituting a commercial and industrial strategy, as well as a diplomatic and military strategy, in all likelihood revolves around the future of television, rebaptized as *home theatre*.

The central instrument reconfiguring the family living room of the supposedly middle-class families who constitute the industrial *demos* will soon be, in fact, a computer turned into a super-television, which will also be an instrument of tele-action and entertainment, as well as a high-definition channel of a new kind, enabling the navigation of video and music databases, by using algorithmic navigation functions to access stocks of 'cultural data'.[25] As for the mobile phone, which can already capture and receive images, it is now becoming a new vehicle for advertising. And the computer, converging with the mobile phone in becoming WiFi, that is, capable of connecting itself wirelessly practically anywhere, will more and more turn into a television able to remotely control domestic and professional processes, as well as military, police, scientific, logistic and consumer processes: this amounts to the generalization and concretization of the *control society* model.

This is why Microsoft (which bought into Thomson Multimedia in 1998, three years after French Prime Minister Alain Juppé had declared that this company was not worth more than a symbolic franc, and that he was ready to sell it for this amount to a Korean industrial conglomerate, which has, since, undergone serious financial difficulties and closed several factories in France) has explicitly aimed since 1997 to control digital television: in that year, Craig Mundie, vice-president of the global corporation, declared that the world contained a billion televisions, enabling just about every consciousness on the planet to be reached, whereas PCs remain and will remain a mode of access limited merely to a section of the populations living in the industrial democracies. It has been known in the United States since at least 1912 that 'trade follows films' (something that European industrialists and governments have at times failed to comprehend), and thus, at very nearly the identical moment that Mundie launched his mission for a new television system technically based on multimedia technology, to be created by Microsoft (in the wake of its Windows Media Player system), Irving Kristol was declaring that the 'missionaries [of the United States] live in Hollywood'.[26]

It is very much a matter of *missions* – that is, of *spiritual war*. Even if this crusade has, since the illegitimate election of George W. Bush, been transformed into a 'conventional' war, and one occurring outside any international legality, the genuine issue for industrial democracies in general, and for Europe in particular, is still to construct their own politics and economy of spirit, capable of opening an era of a new process of individuation: for the European nations, this means revisiting those *pre-individual funds* in which European culture consists, by individuating in accordance with the specific possibilities of this epoch, namely, in accordance with digital technologies and the new industries they make possible, but also in accordance with *unprecedented practices*, which it is a matter of *cultivating*, and which must not be confused in any way with anything that marketing or industrial *design* refers to as 'uses'.

7. The third industrial revolution must be cultural

The programme industries, which have now become inextricably
linked to information and telecommunications technologies (for
example, Radio Skyrock, which systematically integrates, in real
and direct time, mobile phones and web services – and on which
the main advertisers are mobile phone companies[27]), are today the
key element of economic development and international influence,
as well as the main way in which social contacts are maintained.
Now, these industries pose ecological problems just as serious as
those identified at the Rio and Kyoto summits. A global debate
must be organized to investigate without delay the *enormous
problems of mental environments that are* in *disequilibrium and
that* create *disequilibrium*, environments that constitute an industrial development of cognitive, relational and cultural technologies
that aim solely for short-term and unbridled profit.

In this debate, which must also be a battle (that is, which must
be translated into a policy concretely expressed in legislative measures), one priority must be to constitute a *European politics of
spirit* in relation to these concerns, and, on this basis, and more
generally, to define a new industrial model – because, in the epoch
of cultural capitalism, the totality of producer and consumer
behaviour is affected by the need for such a *revolution*. I use the
word 'revolution', here, to the extent that it is a matter of posing
that an epoch has *passed by and become outmoded* [*révolue*], and
in the sense that, if one can speak of a third *industrial revolution*,
then this must also be a matter of a doubly *epokhal* redoubling,
resulting in a correlative *political, social and cultural revolution*.

Faced with the enormous scale of American public investment
in these domains, both direct and indirect (more often than not
through the intermediary of the military), European politics, in its
paucity, remains dumbstruck: the European Commission in 1998
devoted, in total, 0.06 per cent of its budget to audiovisual creation[28] for the whole of the Union, which is one day's worth of
the common agricultural policy, and one third of the assistance
granted to tobacco growers. These figures must be seen in relation
to the statement by the entrepreneur Rupert Murdoch[29] (one of
the main supporters of Tony Blair and his 'third way'), who
declared in Birmingham, during a summit on audiovisual policy

organized by the European Commission, that Europe creates itself more effectively through the media than it does through its currency: this was clearly correct, and was the lesson of the deplorable electoral results of the European election of 13 June 2004. But audiovisual Europe, which is more than a market for Australian, American and Japanese investors, will only be able to maintain itself on the condition that it breaks not only with the American organization of audiovisual production, but with the American industrial model of which this audiovisual production is only a function.

As I have shown elsewhere, the United States was quick to understand the power of audiovisual temporal objects because the way it was confronted with the question of adoption was unlike that of any other nation: America developed an industrial politics projecting the image of the *American 'we'*, which was also a commercial politics projecting the image of the *I* as a *consumer* – the *model of the consumer thus being invented by America*. More than its money or its military might, American power consists in the force of Hollywood images and of the computer programs which it has *conceived* – in its industrial capacity to *produce new symbols* around which models of life are formed. And this is so because, in the *global economic war, conquering markets has become more important than improving productivity* (which Marx could not see, and which Marxism failed to understand), leading to the fact that in the United States culture becomes that culture industry denounced by Horkheimer and Adorno, and the development of this sector of the economy becomes a priority to the point that capitalism develops into cultural hyperindustrialism.

The model of the culture industries developed in the United States, however, insofar as its goal is the mass production of behaviour, inevitably leads to a hyper-synchronization that tends to result in the attenuation of desire: *the object of desire is always* a singularity, and singularity finds itself inexorably eliminated. Now, without desire, there is no longer desire for the *future*. Leroi-Gourhan has shown that a process of adoption constitutes itself less by the sharing of a common past than by the projection of a desire for the future, from a common interpretation of this past, which is itself, anyway, always artificial. This projection is the condition of what Leroi-Gourhan calls *becoming-unified*, which characterizes the constitution of all social groups, and which is in general also a process of enlargement and territorial expansion, in particular through the integration of older social groups into a larger totality: this is what Cleisthenes and Alexander accomplished, each in his own way, and what Leroi-Gourhan describes as the ancient genesis of present-day China, and also what North America organizes with its cultural technologies and culture industries, and it is the inevitable destiny of all human groups. It is also, and finally, the task of a 'European construction' within the framework of an individuation process that has become worldwide.

And if, consequently, such unification could only be produced through the common projection of a desire for the future, then the creation of such a desire must be the absolute political priority for the constitution of any European policy. Now, desire is, firstly, engendered by way of the symbolic. And symbolic production is today, for the great majority of the populations of the industrial democracies, the work of the culture industries. This is why the process of European psychic and collective individuation presupposes the establishment of an industrial politics exceeding the currently dominant model, and presupposes profoundly rethinking the status and function of *new* culture industries, a possibility that has arisen because the digital technical system enables a complete and profound redefinition of the functioning of media.

8. The task of Europe in the division of the West and global individuation

Three years separate us from September 11, a date that carries us well beyond French, European and even American horizons. That day in New York has reshaped the veritable landscape of European 'construction': the world suddenly crystallized and distinguished political, economic *and spiritual* entities in new ways. Europe, North America, Asia, and those one refers to in hasty shorthand as the countries of the South (among these countries are some unclassifiable singularities), and which include those of the Near and Middle East, suddenly find themselves obliged to redefine the nature of their relations.

A major factor within this redefinition has been the sudden clear affirmation of a *schism* at the core of what, until that point, had been designated with the name 'the West', a name under which falls, moreover, almost all of the 'industrial democracies'. This schism seems irreversible. This is not necessarily bad news for those who distinguish themselves in this way: the schism of Christianity eventually permitted its diversification and transformation. It does not mean that Europe and North America must not, in the future, continue to cultivate privileged relations and to cooperate, even to intensify what could thus become an exchange rather than a form of mimetism. Europe must still have expectations of, and learn from, a more sustained exchange with America – but America, too, must learn to *wait* [*attendre*] for others rather than just to drawing [*attirant*] them in. And, just as Nietzsche thought the future of Germany by projecting it on to the level of Europe, thereby denationalizing it, so too Europe can only think itself by thinking of the global future, and by thinking itself *in* becoming-planetary, in the sense that the process of European psychic and collective individuation can today only occur within a much vaster process of individuation, one that is now manifestly that of planetary humanity: most importantly, this is not a matter of developing a new Eurocentrism.

On the contrary, the future of Europe passes through the reaffirmation of its critical power. Europe cannot inaugurate the process of individuation in which it must consist by seeking its 'essence', its 'identity', or the meaning of its 'cultural heritage'. And the question is not that of knowing what Europe *is*. Europe is not: it becomes.[30] And like all psycho-social individuation, it is a fiction – a fiction which only lasts as long as people believe in it. It is a process of adoption which, insofar as it effectively engenders adoption, is also an individuation, but which only exists as the projection of a future remaining always to come, and thus a future which only exists in the mode of this projection.[31] Europe is obviously constituted by its 'heritage', which is its force. But this is only a *force* as a power *of the future* – that is, as the capacity to *break with that decadent, exhausted and self-destructive state of affairs* to which the industrial model of the twentieth century has led, a model which shaped the American way of life, and which became the model for every industrial democracy, at a time when they were still prosperous. Free from cultural baggage [*incantations patrimoniales*], but still supported by its past, the future of Europe lies in its critique, without concessions to an industrial model which is collapsing, and it therefore lies in the invention of another model.

Europe must, therefore, invent its own political *and industrial* project: any specifically political project cannot be distinguished independently of a correspondingly specific industrial project, and this is not merely a question of strategic industrial choices, so that, for example, it might be considered necessary to reinforce European aeronautics, or develop a European industrial software, and so on.[32] Such ideas may be of interest, but they are not relevant to the questions here being pursued: the project of conceiving a new industrial *model* requires a complete rethinking of the organization of production and consumption, and in particular requires *putting a cancellation date* on the imperatives of that particular form of subsistence referred to as 'development', whether 'sustainable' or otherwise.

In this context, Europe must without doubt engage in significant dialogue with China, that immense country which will soon become fully industrial, but which also inherits an extremely long history.

9.   On the construction process: the struggle against addiction

There is a *catastrophe*, in terms of the political decadence of capitalist democracies, a catastrophe in the sense that a new industrial model, and *by the same token a cultural, and therefore political, model*, must be conceived and implemented, and this must take place at a continental level – that of Europe – as an entirely new notion of capitalism-become-cultural, on a worldwide scale. *Within the current capitalism typical of control societies, the function of culture has been reduced to socializing production by standardizing consumer behaviour, culture thereby becoming the agent par excellence of this control.* Now, as I have said elsewhere, and as I will return to in what follows, this control is an exploitation of libidinal energy that *exhausts* this energy, and it is in this way that the industrial model emerging from twentieth-century modernity reaches its limit, particularly in Europe and principally in wealthy Europe.

Encountering this limit, which constitutes an immense danger, is also a chance: it is the chance to invent, *at the moment when the mutation of the technical system makes possible new arrangements*, another social model, which could foreshadow a new stage of becoming of the industrial democracies of the entire world. *No Logo* by Naomi Klein, and *The Age of Access* by Jeremy Rifkin, have had enormous worldwide success, and first of all in North America. This is not an epiphenomenon, but a sign pointing to the fact that *another way of life is being sought*. Europeans, in the search for their new story [*histoire*], must be *interpreters* of these signs and, as such, inventors of an industrial organization constituted in the theatre of psychic and collective individuation, that is, they must create genuine *modes of existence*, to counter the reduction, by the obsolete industrial model, of all existence to *modes of subsistence*, and in the end to ersatz, stereotypical, existences.[33] Leroi-Gourhan saw this coming in 1965, when he wrote:

> Our society's emotional ration is already largely made up of ethnographic accounts of groups that have ceased to exist – Sioux Indians, cannibals, sea pirates – forming the framework for responsiveness systems of great poverty and arbitrariness. One may wonder what the level of reality of these superficially sketched images will be when their creators are drawn from a fourth generation of people remote-controlled in their audiovisual contacts with a fictitious world.[34]

In fact, forty years after these strikingly lucid lines were written, the 'superficially sketched images' [*images sommairement emaillées*, more literally: images summarily stuffed with straw – trans.] have given way to reality television and the pseudo-experiences on offer in American malls, which Jeremy Rifkin described thus:

> The developers of the West Edmonton megamall envisioned bringing the culture of the world into a giant indoor space, where it could be commodified in the form of bits of entertainment to delight and amuse visitors and stimulate the desire to buy. [...] One can ride a rickshaw; go onboard a full-length replica of the

Santa María; pet farm animals in the petting zoo; be photographed
with a live lion, tiger, or jaguar; and take part in an 'authentic'
Mongolian barbecue.[35]

And Leroi-Gourhan in a certain way anticipates the mall and,
more generally, the consequences of cultural capitalism described
by Rifkin, as well as reality television and the most recent forms
of tourism, when he offers the following prognosis:

> Ten generations from now a writer selected to produce social fiction
> will probably be sent on a 'renaturation' course in a park a corner
> of which he or she will have to till with a plough copied from a
> museum exhibit and pulled by a horse borrowed from a zoo. He
> or she will cook and eat the family meal at the family table, orga-
> nize neighbourhood visits, enact a wedding, sell cabbages from a
> market stall to other participants in the same course, and learn
> anew how to relate the ancient writings of Gustave Flaubert to the
> meagrely constituted reality.[36]

In all these situations, it is matter of 'stimulating their desire
for consumption'. But the reality is that this submission of existence to the imperatives of global subsistence (and of an economic
development which can only widen the gap between producers
and consumers in view of intensifying their exchanges) leads to
an enormous disbanding [*débandade*]: the moral and spiritual
crisis afflicting our world is nothing other than the very disturbing
symptom of this disbanding. Every human being is constituted by
his or her *intimate and original* relation to *singularity* and, first of
all, by the knowledge that he or she has of *their* singularity, of the
necessity of their being-unique, and this is why herdish behaviours, almost like the image we have of human cloning, provoke
a tremendous malaise among those who endure them, a dangerous
dissatisfaction with oneself and a profound loss of belief in the
future, the paradox being that this malaise and this feeling of loss
in fact reinforce the herdish tendency itself, through a retroactive
loop constituting a vicious circle. It is this circle that must be
broken: this *and decadence and the obligations it creates for us as
political task*.

Cultural capitalism exploits that vicious circle consisting in
the fact that consumption and the resulting herdishness induce

anxiety, an anxiety which is therefore caught within a feedback loop that merely reinforces consumer behaviour, behaviour that tries in vain to *compensate* for this anxiety: such a pattern is typical of an addictive cycle. *Addiction is the effective reality of the dominant industrial model.* This addiction is an annihilation of the subject of the addiction by the object of addiction, that is, an absorption of his or her existence by that which, here, tries to maintain and augment mechanisms of subsistence: consumption is the everyday mode of subsistence, but industrial consumption is a hypertrophied form of consumption, to the point that it becomes an object of addiction. Now, just as an *unlimited* exploitation of natural resources by industrial investment is impossible, so too a society which, by completely submitting to subsistence imperatives, nullifies the existence of those who compose it, is doomed to collapse.[37] This is true for everyone, consciously or otherwise, as a *global process of degradation*, where consciousness (conscious time) has become a commodity, the price of which is calculable in the marketplace, a commodity about which negotiations take place every day in terms of 'supply' and 'demand'.[38]

This is why, in relation to the idea, irresolute and dry, abstract and formal, inscribed within an old but still dominant industrial model, of what is called 'European construction', created through administrative measures and various exhortations, from 'directives' which in the eyes of Europeans fail to support any kind of project – no more than does the euro, and this is what became obvious on 13 June 2004, the current president of the Union being, furthermore, not one likely to make changes in this regard – it is a matter of unleashing a process that creates a *rupture* with this exhausted epoch. This must be, precisely, the process of a new European *individuation*, itself inscribed in a planetary process. A new history, following the *catastrophe*, must establish the conditions of a new epoch of Western psychic and collective individuation, differentiating itself from what until now has been the industrial and democratic West in its totality, localizing itself in Europe, replaying *through the projection of a reinvented industrial future* the individuation of *pre-individual funds* which this continent, a geographical and historical entity, supports on its soil and through its inhabitants.

As for that new and gigantic planetary immensity of which September 11 was at once the vertiginous date of birth, the drawing of new frontiers, and a *hold on the unconscious*, how might we broach this, given that everything appears to have become utterly unpredictable insofar as it is all utterly *irrational*? The only possible approach to such a question consists in *affirming*, through an uncompromising critique, the possibility of a gap within the horizon-to-come, constituting a motive of *desire* and, as such, a genuine *reason*. An irrational society is one that demotivates those who constitute it – and this is what today provokes the unlimited industrial exploitation of libidinal energy. This is what I have elsewhere called 'disbanding'. And it is what I call here the decadence of industrial democracies.

10. Political shame

The 'French malady', if there is one – what certain people have in a very dated and laboured fashion felt it necessary to call France's 'decline' – is a version of that malady of the *we* afflicting those industrial societies referred to as democracies: it is not a national decline, but the decadence of a planetary epoch and of a political and economic model that has today become globalized. No doubt each of these democracies has 'its' decadence. But this is much more a matter of a process of the *disindividuation of industrial democracies in general*, a process through which these democracies are connected to a series of exchanges, products, symbols and behavioural models, and forming in totality a process of planetary reach – and hence a process which, equally, comes to be *exported* into countries that are neither democratic nor industrial, but nonetheless find themselves carried along into their own decline.

Speaking of the decline of France is in fact a way of masking the decadence that is actually the source of this discourse, and it is a way of preventing reflection on the decadence of the West and of the democratic and industrial model which it has engendered. There are numerous versions of this kind of discourse, the so-called 'decline of France' being merely one of them. It is as a function of our capacity to will a new epoch of the individuation process – that is, to *invent* it, and to thus stimulate a psychic and collective individuation process – that the critique of decadence may interrupt a process that, if it merely takes its course, will lead to a worldwide degeneration of humanity. The fear of speaking in terms of degeneration, and the mask that the theme of national decline constitutes, are what, preventing the critique of the decadent model of industrial democracy, in turn prevents the renewal of political thought and decision, and thereby engenders discredit: political miscreance, or the disbelief in politics, is a political cynicism which takes the form of neither believing in nor wanting to believe in what might lie beyond this decadence. Decadence is that which supposes in advance that everything is *already* finished.

The necessary *leap* [*saut*] from the national to the planetary – without which no political thought is possible today, in passing through the continentality of our '*petit cap*', such that it must become a localized individuation of a renewed industrial future – is only possible by in the first place rethinking that global decadence common to all industrial democracies, and the consequences of which are being exported everywhere else: this leap is perhaps nothing other than a *jumpstart* [*sursaut*].

(Certainly not all countries are industrial democracies, and this is never something to rejoice about, but neither should these regions be submitted to a destiny of resembling us, suiting us, or overwhelming us: these countries, being neither industrial nor democratic, are for the most part places containing great suffering, where it is very difficult to survive, where in some cases brutality reigns, and where the future appears condemned to disappear into a black hole – even if, as everyone knows, and which has been a long time coming, China, which, like Europe, is a very old individuation process, of which the cultural pre-individual funds are monumental, might still hold great surprises in store, both good ones, as its cinema causes us to think, and bad ones, to the degree that *hyper-exponential* rates of growth characterize the curves by which one measures both its 'development' and the immensity of its problems.)

In this context one must conclude that, unfortunately, the people of France, and the French political apparatus, from April 2002 up until June 2004, and in spite of the extreme importance of the last election, have yet to change in any way either their discourse, their attitudes, their practices or their non-projects. They have opened no space for thought; nor for debate. Social anxiety, often despair, deviance, and at times suicidal behaviours, the causes of which remain partially mysterious and in every case multiple, have nevertheless been found to be dangerously aggravated.[39] No lesson has been learned, either by the government or by the opposition: having already been stunned by the realization they had managed to hold on to power, however narrowly, they both managed to forget, within a matter of weeks, and as quickly as they had discovered it, the overwhelming decay revealed on this infamous 21 April 2002, and for which, until 28 March 2004, no pacifying rattle would appear. They therefore maintain their silence and their reserve, giving an impression of humility and decency, indeed of shame, the appearance of being reflective, but this appearance is, in reality, *completely illusory*.

It might have been hoped that following these warning shots fired at the entire political class – for such were these national elections – the opposition parties at least would in some way, at last, have begun to approach the true questions yet to be asked in the debate about the future of Europe. This interval, however, from 28 March (which was a warning to the entire political scene and not merely to the French government) until 13 June (the date of the European election, but an election which was clearly also of national importance), was not only characterized by an absence of political reflection. During this brief but decisive period, and beyond the usual clichés and egocentric chattering which imagines itself to be 'strategic', there also took place a proliferating media commotion, designed to 'occupy the ground', but in a way that was unusually demagogical and irresponsible. Yet there was a distinct failure to imagine that it might be necessary to make possible a new collective intelligence of our situation, grounded in the analysis of these very serious failures.

As for the current public institutions, having failed to propose a European policy, they decided instead to launch, most noticeably on the walls and trains of the Paris metro, a publicity campaign in the style of mass advertising, a campaign that was not only deaf and blind to what was heralded by the so-called 'anti-pub' movement, but also unrelentingly contributed to the growth of every kind of misery: economic, symbolic, libidinal and political. It is thus that the European parliament introduced, in partnership with CIDEM (Civisme et Démocratie), a series of advertisements on radio, on roads, in cinemas, on buses and on the metro. And thus throughout France one could read posters inscribed with the following text:

> WHO IS GOING TO DEFEND CONSUMERS? YOU [*VOUS*].
> June 13 – Let's vote [*votons*]
> For the European Parliament
> The protection of consumers: our representatives
> are working for you.

It is impossible not to be struck by the *admission* contained within this slogan: advertising is being used to address those who must be called to behave as citizens, but who at the same time are placed in the position of consumers, as if they alone were responsible for their situation – that is, as if the political organizations have *nothing* to say to them about this situation itself, except that it is an immutable fact. And it is a strange use indeed of the personal pronoun, '*vous*', a usage that does not correspond to the subsequent conjugation of the verb in the first person ('*votons*'), since the latter makes its appeal to a *we*.

Such an address does not seem *capable* of speaking to a *we* and in fact gives the impression that it is unconcerned with such a *we*: rather, it addresses itself *to the mass*. This is not merely a matter of grammatical awkwardness by the public relations consultants entrusted with this campaign, and to whom political institutions have delegated their responsibilities. Through this European parliamentary bureaucracy, in collaboration with the French government, Europe and the French state address themselves to the mass of consumers – to whom the electors are *in fact reduced* – while saying to them that they must protect themselves, and that they can only do so while *remaining*, at the very moment that they *vote*, within their status as consumers, something which is thus *performatively*[40] reaffirmed by this billboard, as though it were a matter of an ineluctable fate.

This billboard [*affiche publicitaire*] is therefore not a *political* poster [*affiche politique*]: discourse or thought, that is, the critique of what is and what becomes, has given way to public relations [*communication*], and the *demos* disappears into political consumerism or, rather, into a consumerism which is in fact anti-political, that is, self-destructive.

To prevent any misunderstanding, however, I must immediately add: this is not a matter of condemning consumption; nor of condemning the original meaning of 'consumerism', which initially referred to the movement in defence of consumers. Not merely insofar as we are living beings, but also insofar as we are social beings, that is, economic beings, we consume, we have consumed, and we will consume – and, inasmuch as we are consumers, we are in *need* of being protected, and thus we need organizations to protect us in this way. Consumption is the condition of industrial activity, and no exit from this situation is any longer on the horizon: the age of technics will never be overcome, contrary to delusions which may be spread far and wide. It is no longer a matter of condemning publicity as such. Even if it is necessary to contain its excesses, which moreover threaten it directly and mechanically, industrial innovation clearly requires organs of communication and of the promotion of the new products in which it consists.

11. The consistence of the *vita activa*

It *is*, on the other hand, a matter of condemning consumer*ism*, defined here as the reduction of the citizen and, more generally, of the psychic and collective individual, to the status of pure consumer, that is, to his or her conditions of subsistence, such that his or her conditions of existence are annihilated. It is thus a matter of *struggling against the hegemony of an industrial division of social roles* that has become obsolete, and against which consumer organizations must themselves struggle more and more – and, in particular, wherever industrial objects involve *practices* irreducible to mere *usages*, that is, irreducible to that becoming 'worn out' [*usure*] which leads to the disposability [*jetabilité*] of that of which it makes use, a usage submitting the object to pure and simple utility.

I am talking here about those industrial objects that one refers to as equipment, that one treats as tools, but that have an *instrumental* vocation that is not merely utilitarian: thus it is that the tool utilizes [*utilise*] the world, to which it is nevertheless also a mode of access; the instrument *instructs* [*instruits*] this world, *makes* the world – given that any tool, precisely insofar as it is a mode of access, can become an instrument, like a chisel in the hands of the sculptor, but can also become the opposite.

Today, a vast instrumentality has begun to take place traversing all the equipment issued from the three preceding industrial revolutions, and of which a politics, at once industrial and cultural, is henceforth required: this instrumentality opens the possibility of a new age of symbolic exchange.

The conditions of existence, insofar as they are irreducible to subsistence alone, are *symbolic activities* – even those which, since the Greeks, have been conceived as the rights and duties of the citizen – activities which weave the *consistence* of what Hannah Arendt called the *vita activa*. The question of this consistence is the subject of the following chapter, a chapter that demonstrates that the *loss of individuation* is a *loss of consistence*, a loss which, in the course of the twentieth century, has extended not only to the modes of production of subsistence but to those modes of consumption through which existence has been denied (disindividuated).

In other words, the submission of existence to standardized behavioural models of consumption follows the process of proletarianization that had begun in the nineteenth century with the standardization of modes of production. The consumer is the new proletarian figure, and the proletariat, very far from disappearing, is a condition from which it has become nearly impossible to escape.

2

Belief and Politics

In the Capitalist Age

. . . not to envisage power from a juridical point of view, but from a technological one.[1]

Michel Foucault

What I relate is the history of the next two centuries. I describe what is coming, what cannot fail to come: *the advent of nihilism.*

Friedrich Nietzsche[2]

. . . and when you have to embark on the sea, you emigrants, you, too, are compelled to by this – a *faith*!

Friedrich Nietzsche[3]

1. Capitalism: a specific epoch of the Western grammatization process

The central idea of the preceding chapter may be summarized: we live in decadent times for democracy, a decadence entailed by the becoming-consumerist of industrial societies. The advent of consumerism is inscribed within that process of social transformation that, since Marx, one calls capitalism. Capitalism, which during the twentieth century became cultural capitalism, now tends to liquidate politics properly speaking, that is, first of all, to liquidate the public power of the state, but, more generally, it tends to liquidate the psychic and collective individuation process through which singularities are formed and exchanged – this process being itself the experience of its own singularity, that is, of its *incalcu-lability*, or, again, of the irreducibility of its future to mere becom-ing. Now, having become cultural and at the same time hyper-industrial, capitalism is today *essentially computational*, and as such tends to eliminate those singularities that resist the calculability of all values on the market of economic exchange.

This tendency towards liquidating politics, and the individua-tion in which politics consists, must be fought, but without holding on to an obsolete idea of politics, that is, one founded on the discourse of 'resistance': holding on to such a politics could only mean becoming ensnared in one more delusion. One must struggle against this tendency by *inventing* rather than by resisting. Resistance can only ever be *reactive* and, as such, it belongs to *nihilism* – in the Nietzschean sense of these words. 'Politics' – if this word must be retained, which is not certain – must be resolutely, immediately and conjointly, but *distinctly*, the *inven-tion* of a *scientific and technological* politics, an *industrial* politics, and a *cultural* politics, but the meaning of this last word, 'culture', must be completely revisited: this is a new task, a task that precedes all others. It is in this way alone that politics can and must elaborate a new model of the industrial organization of societies.

Combating a *tendency* within a process means, first of all, thinking this process as the articulation of a *dual* [*double*] ten-dency, which is what makes it dynamic. In other words, this process is a *conjunction* of tendencies, such that one is indispens-able to the maintenance of the other. This dynamic organization constituted as a dual tendency, as the conjunction of two compos-ing tendencies, is a structure inscribed at the very heart of indi-viduation, and still more as what confers upon it its movement, that is, also, since this is what drives it, it is what constitutes its motive, a motive which is therefore always already dual and, as such, a *duplicity* [*duplice*: the translation as 'duplicity' contains an echo not only of duplicitousness but also of duplication and multiplicity – trans.].

The process of individuation, in fact, always already tends towards unification, towards becoming-one, that is, in-divisible (as the word '*in-dividual*' literally signifies), and yet it never ceases its becoming, and is therefore never actually completed [*achevé*] and always remains to come. The individual individuating itself is living – and this is also true of civilizations, which can be 'mortal' only to this extent – and when the individual reaches completion, this is because they have died. This incompletion [*inachèvement*] is, as such, an irreducible trait of individu-*ation* insofar as it is a process, a process which, as the *becoming-other* of the one, is also a *becoming-multiple* of this one.

The in-dividual, in short, never reaches the state of being in-dividual. And this is why it is necessary to reason in terms of *processes*, rather than in terms of stasis or states. This originary contradiction within individuation, that tension constituting it as its dual motive, is what Simondon thinks when he characterizes individuation as a *metastable* equilibrium, that is, as a process that is in movement to the extent that it is: on the one hand, partially stable, close to equilibrium and able to maintain its form (as for instance a whirlpool maintains itself within a flowing current, while nevertheless deforming and evolving); and yet, on the other hand, partially unstable, insofar as this form never ceases to become other than what it is.

To put this in another way, *a tendency is never bad in itself*: it is the condition of the tendency to which it *seems* to oppose itself, while in reality it never ceases to compose with it. In this way, tendencies form a transductive relation, a relation which constitutes its terms such that one term cannot exist without the other. It is possible, however, that at times runaway tendencies can form, which, becoming *hegemonic*, tend to eliminate the contrary tendency and, as a result, can destroy the relation through which they constituted themselves, and, in so doing, may destroy themselves.

Beyond that 'rationalization' described by Weber, and the separation of capital and labour described by Marx, capitalism is the expression of a tendency towards the *mechanical externalization* [*extériorisation machinique*] of that which characterizes the singularities composing the process of individuation; and, as such, it is the *mechanized epoch* of what, in *De la misère symbolique 1*, I have called *grammatization*.[4] Nevertheless this tendency, as mechanical exteriorization, has the effect of producing a standardization and a formalization, submitting everything that it formalizes to *calculability*. As such, it pursues rationalization (in Weber's sense), and tends thereby also to *synchronize the diachronies* in which these singularities consist. This synchronization, insofar as it is mechanized and calculated, and makes conscious time [*temps des consciences*] into a commodity, is nevertheless a *hyper*-synchronization, and in this way it seems that capitalism opposes singularities.

And yet, beyond the fact that diachrony is always constituted on the basis of synchrony, *singularities can and must be recast* [*rejouer*] *on a new plane in this capitalist and hyper-industrial stage of exteriorization* – failing which, it is the capitalist process itself that will collapse, an outcome that would not in any way be desirable: such an event would without doubt be premature (that is, the individuation of capitalism has not advanced to the point of being capable of giving way to a new organization) and, were it to take place, would inevitably result both in innumerable wars that would immediately become global, and in immense chaos, if not indeed the disappearance of the human species. This is not to say that capitalism is an eternal form of human organization: such forms do not exist. Human history is a process of individuation that never ceases inventing new forms of organization, and for this reason we still do not know how, despite two centuries of evolutionary thought, to conceive the fact that we must now relearn how to think, that is, also, how to *decide*.

Grammatization, which lies at the origin of the invention of the figure of the citizen, was in that epoch an *expropriation* of singularities through the exteriorization of their characteristics, leading to the liquidation of tribes and their replacement by *demes*, and to the transfer of the most intense points of singularity from the tribal level (represented by the chief) to the level of the isonomic political individual – that is, such that *each* individual constituted a singularity in law, of which the *polis* would be, as a process, the ceaseless expression, renewed by this law and as the theatre of its individuation. Nevertheless, the social becoming induced by grammatization, in the form of the birth of the *polis* (that is, the process of Western individuation), was already, at the same time, the site of a conflict, expressed in the struggle between sophistry and philosophy – that is, a conflict about the status of mnemo-technics, which I have called ortho-graphy,[5] and which Plato called *hypomnesis* and *logography*, and to which he believed must be *opposed* what he called *anamnesis*. During this period that gave birth to the West, therefore, the question was to know what interpretation to give to that form of grammatization that was unfolding at that time.

Today, this question remains intact. And this is why the analysis of the metaphysical blockage that Platonic philosophy has constituted, *on this point in particular*, is also the *preliminary* requirement for the critique of capitalism. (I develop these points in detail in *Technics and Time*, and will do so further in the fourth volume, *Symboles et diaboles*.)

2. Capitalism and belief

To combat the tendency towards the liquidation of politics is, therefore, to combat a tendency of capitalism such as it is, an *epoch* of Western psychic and collective individuation. Because the 'globalization' of capitalism, *that is, also, its de-Westernization*, is a component of this individuation that pursues a grammatization process *at a planetary level*, a process which requires *epokhal* redoubling.

In brief, it is not a matter of *opposing* the capitalist process but, on the contrary, of enabling it to see out its term, that is, of avoiding its self-destruction, and hence permitting its transformation, and perhaps thereby engendering, some day, a wholly other organization of individuation. Capitalism is a process of transformation of which we are ignorant of the end. It had a beginning, and one day it will come to an end – but we have no way of knowing where or when this will occur. The only way of living with this process is to make it possible for it to follow itself out, until that moment when, coming to completion, it could perhaps engender a new process, of which we remain utterly ignorant, because it is incalculable. Insofar as it is an *epoch* of psychic and collective individuation, capitalism has been preceded by a Western, precapitalist past, and it will be followed by a future which is already no longer simply Western, and which perhaps may not be capitalist: individuation is the constitution of the future as the opening of the indeterminate *to which all existing singularity bears witness*, which is singular precisely and uniquely in this sense, and to which it bears witness as that which, in it, *consists beyond that which exists and which is its future* – consistence, which shows itself through the singularity of that which exists and which, as such, is the singularity that must be protected.

Even though we are inevitably completely ignorant of it, we must therefore pose that this future, which does not exist, is what consists through all that which, as irreducible to mere subsistence, exists, and which, as existence, *singularly aims at* (that is, in a way itself indeterminable and as such diachronic) this consistence of individuation insofar as it remains *structurally* to come and as such indeterminate. And this is also why the critique of contemporary capitalism, insofar as it is the hegemony of *subsistence* and the negation of *existence*, must pose the question of *consistence* and, as such, of the *belief* constituting it, that is, in which it consists.

As such, the consumerist transformation of industrial democracies, the critical analysis of which must constitute the basis of a renewal of the psychic and collective individuation process, must be interpreted in relation to a process of becoming older than that of *the division of social classes*. This is what Marx was unable to think, because he failed to fully grasp the consequences of the appearance of mnemo-technics and mnemo-technologies, which are the basis for both ancient and recent developments of the grammatization process characterizing Western becoming. These mnemo-techniques and mnemo-technologies, which constitute the characteristic pre-individual funds of the psychic and collective individuation process in which the West consisted, at present form the basis, as digital technology, of a cultural capitalism that is both hyper-industrial and planetary. Marxist analyses see the issue of mnemo-technics and mnemo-technologies in terms of the relation to the notion of 'superstructure',[6] but in fact hyper-industrial capitalism consists in the *impossibility of distinguishing* infrastructure from superstructure – and for this reason the critique of such a capitalism must also be a critique of Marx's philosophy.

I will refer, then, to that in which an individuation process *consists*, and in this chapter I will attribute great importance to this verb – '*to consist*': that which *consists* is not that which *exists*; it is that which gives meaning [*sens*] (its direction and its movement, or its *driving force* [*force motrice*]) to what exists, without reducing itself to this existing. Existing is a *fact*. But existing only consists as that which *surpasses* [*dépasse*] its *factuality* [*fait*]. The consistence of a fact is what the process of individuation, wherever it occurs, is capable of *projecting*. This raises the question of what I have elsewhere called *retentional and protentional systems*. In effect, the process of individuation is *temporal* and, as such, is *woven* with retentions and protentions, just like that temporal object analysed by Husserl.[7]

In the course of the Western individuation process, consistence was for a long time essentially established as the *religious* belief constituted by the Church, insofar as it formed a retentional and protentional system – and thus through discourse on the absolute past, God the father, as well as on the absolute future, his son – a system lasting until the advent of the Enlightenment and the French Revolution (which both foreshadowed the industrial revolution and constituted its conditions of possibility) trans-formed this religious belief into *political and social* belief, that is, into belief in *progress*. This was, then, the beginning of the *dis-absolutization of the past and of the future* and, as such, the liquidation of the discourse of being, that is, of the ontotheo-logico-political discourse *which constituted the division of social classes* (nobility, clergy, third estate). It entailed, as well, confront-ing an experience of becoming as 'disenchantment of the world', but also, first of all, as a discourse of emancipation: of the *trans-formation* of the world (of the world as *becoming*), and not only the *interpretation* of the world (of the world as *being*).

Today, belief in progress, insofar as it is technological and, *cor-relatively*, social and political, has collapsed (a fact which then becomes translated into a dangerous divorce between science – become technoscience – and society). Now, this collapse is also a *tendential and detemporalizing process: there tends to be less consciousness of the past, and there also tends to be less of a feeling for the future* – and, as such, there is an attenuation of the possibility of having an *experience* properly speaking. This is the non-epoch of what I have called disorientation,[8] in which the doubly epochal redoubling fails to occur, or, in other words, a non-epoch in which society disadjusts itself from the technical system, and where this disadjustment is already, in itself, a loss of time. But the technical system, itself tending to become a 'real time' system, and tending to become a system of completely calculated and hyper-synchronized time, thus combines these *two processes of detemporalization* that together lead to a loss of individuation – something already expressed in a slogan typical of young people at the end of the twentieth century: '*no future*'.

3. Time and calculation in the capitalist age

The impossibility of a doubly epochal redoubling implies that *technology and society have become divorced*. This is what Jean-François Lyotard believed it necessary to call 'the end of grand narratives' (that is, of all narratives of emancipation through progress), and hence it has been defined as a supposedly 'postmodern' age. With the collapse of the idea of progress, an idea that can never be anything other than a belief, it is the very belief in politics that collapses. Some of the causes of this collapse, moreover, are intrinsic to the becoming of the Western process of psychic and collective individuation itself, causes that are thus inscribed within it from the beginning, but there are also other causes, arising specifically from the more recent epoch of capitalist development.

These are the two historical levels that require analysis if we are to understand why it has not been possible to accomplish the doubly epochal redoubling.[9] If this doubly epochal redoubling – through which a new epoch of civilization is attained, following the upheaval of the technical system – fails to occur today, this is because, confronted with the fact that the instability of technical becoming has become chronic, a situation completely unprecedented in human history, psycho-social individuation does not succeed in reaching the point of *inventing an epoch of individuation capable of integrating this techno-logical hyper-diachronicity as its motive*. At this point, then, with technological evolution having become incessant and therefore hyper-diachronic (that is, technological obsolescence is involved in a process of continual acceleration), the paradoxical result is that societies and the individuals composing them regress to their most archaic stages, and withdraw to a state of herdish hyper-synchronization in which they become disindividuated. The diachronicity of society and its members is defined only by its objects, and these support usages the behavioural models of which are now formalized and standardized by marketing, creating a situation in which obsolescence prevents *time* from transforming these usages into *practices*.

Beyond a thousand other explanations – of which Freud offered the most important, when he studied tendencies in terms of the life and death drives, and the way in which in the twentieth century the conflict of these tendencies plays out *as the age of crowds and masses in their relation to technological explosion* – the impossibility of effecting a leap into a psycho-social individuation capable of integrating techno-logical diachronicity can be tied to two reasons, echoing two extremities of the history of Western individuation: on one side the birth of philosophy, and on the other side the becoming-hyper-industrial of capitalism:

• Firstly, there is a *metaphysical blockage* inscribed in Western psychic and collective individuation from its earliest beginnings: the repression by the religious and lay clergy of the constitutivity of technics, a repression that continues today. (I treat this in successive volumes of *Technics and Time*, and merely recall it here.)
• Secondly, those powers dominating the contemporary capitalist process cultivate political obsolescence, in order to facilitate and accelerate the capitalist process through a technical intelligence *pragmatically* emancipated from Western metaphysics – and which makes capitalism, as it were, factually 'deconstructive', but where this 'deconstruction' in fact becomes a destruction, resulting in what I have characterized as the decadence of industrial democracies. (This is what I treat here.)

The question underlying all these processes is that of belief, such that the death of God, and the development of economic and managerial theories of trust, as *calculated trust*,[10] have rendered this question both crucial and unthinkable.

Before going any further, I must restate that I am not at all condemning calculation, not even the calculation of the possibility of constituting and reinforcing trust or confidence. I have shown, on the contrary, and counter to the thesis defended by Heidegger in *Being and Time*, that no temporality of *Dasein* (that is, of existence, that is, also, of any psycho-social process) is possible (no relation to the future and no trust in this future is possible) which does not pass through calculation. And there is a *history* of this temporality (which is a history of individuation) *to the degree* that there is a history of *calculation*. In the West, this history of calculation becomes that of grammatization.

On the other hand, I argue that the *reduction* of trust (and of time, that is, of belief in a future) to pure calculation, which would be capable therefore of eliminating everything incalculable, is what *radically destroys all trust*, because it destroys all *possibility of believing*: all possibility of believing in the indetermination of the future, in the future as indeterminate and in this indetermination as a *chance*, an *opening* to the future as to its im-probability, that is, to the future as *irreducibly singular*.

Because this BELIEF is the form of the relation to TIME, or to time as relation (to those 'extases' which constitute it, as the past, present and future of individuation, both psychic and collective, and everything this entails). Now, because trust is only possible within a horizon of *belief* that surpasses it, calculating trust is necessarily self-destructive: it is a denial of the future, that is, of time. As for the *belief* that *inspires* trust, this can and must also take the form of *fear*. This is what the Greek word, *elpis*, means: expectation (that is, protention), at once hope and fear.[11] Insofar as it is indeterminate, time, like the future, can only be feared *as much as* it is hoped for, *to the degree* that it permits hope. But with the decomposition of those forces and tendencies constituting a process of individuation, hope and fear come to oppose one another and thus decompose. Hope gives way to resentment [*ressentiment*], and fear gives way to the future-panic [*devenir-panique*] of the mass age.

Such a form of capitalism results, as the rationalization of society, in the reduction of trust to calculation. It is no longer, however, a matter of condemning this historical process, which does in fact open new stakes for humanity. If the stakes opened by the development of the capitalist process call for *combat*, this must not be conducted against the process of which capitalism is the bearer, that process which pursues grammatization, but rather against that which, in this process, threatens this process itself, as its limits and its contradictions. Capitalism is before anything else an age of *credit*. Insofar as it is credit, capitalism presupposes a belief in the future – a belief in a future which may be anticipated, and therefore a future which can be calculated, but also a belief in a future which, because it can only be *absolutely* indeterminate and open (failing which there would be no future) always *exceeds* the calculations that capital can count on [*escompter*]. This is why the current stage of capitalism, which is hyper-industrial to the degree that it is hyper-computational, insofar as it is capable of transforming *everything* into numbers, is encountering its limit and entering into a zone of very great danger.

The belief that the capitalist process needs is at its core an-economic, *if* one understands by *economy* that which can be reduced to an economy *of subsistence*. If one does not want to understand economy in this way, if one does not want to see it reduced in this way merely to subsistence, one must pose that *belief* is only *economic* in the sense that it is a *libidinal, symbolic and spiritual economy* incapable of being reduced to the computation of capital: it is a matter of an *economy of singularity*, which calls for a *politics of singularities* – something that could only emerge from combat.

4. Combat in capitalism, capitalism as combat, combat against capitalist totalitarianism, and the question of the best (*ariston*)

The absolute indetermination of the future, that is, of what an individuation process can project as protention, is the encounter of this process with *its own* singularity, but which, mostly, is concretely expressed only as an experience of singularity that this process encounters in terms of what is *not* its own, but rather that of another with which or whom it co-individuates (and forms a *we*), including the other *thing*, which is, most of the time, that through which it is possible to encounter that other with whom it may be possible to form a *we*.[12]

Singularity, then, is the motive of all protention, and protention is the individuation process dynamically projecting itself. This singularity, furthermore, can never be reduced to the particularity of a whole of which it would be nothing more than a part calculable on the basis of this whole itself. Affirming all this, however, does not mean that it is a matter of *opposing* calculation to belief; nor, more generally, that it is a matter of thinking through oppositions – it is, rather, a matter of thinking through composition.

But this does not mean that an individuation process must not *oppose* – that is, *combat* – that which, in the expression of the tendencies that *weave* the *dynamic* of individuation, leads to the *decomposition* of these tendencies. This question of combat is central, and must be entirely re-elaborated in terms of politics. All individuation is a combat. All politics is a combat. All existence is a combat. Politics and existence are forms of combat against their *base* [*vile*] tendencies – that is, against the attempt by tendencies to become hegemonic and to destroy the counter-tendencies which constitute them, and which they constitute, a destruction that always results in a *simplification* of existence, dragging it down to the level of mere subsistence conditions. All existence must always struggle against that which, *in itself*, tends to *renounce* existence. And all politics must struggle against that which, in psycho-social individuation, *spontaneously* inclines towards this same renunciation.

The renunciation of existence is a renunciation of becoming-other as future, that is, as *elevation*.

The psycho-social individual that one most commonly calls 'man' is a being for whom the fundamental movement is to elevate itself: it is thus defined by its conquest of the upright stance, of erect posture, which is also and in the same movement, its conquest of technicity, that is, of a mobility which passes through its artefactualization, through its *ars* and *metiers*, its knowledge and its power. As a process of individuation, this conquest as elevation is never complete: human beings may launch themselves towards Mars and accelerate beyond 'escape velocity', or write *Un coup de dés jamais n'abolira le hazard* [*A Throw of the Dice Will Never Abolish Chance* – Mallarmé], they may teach at the Collège de France, or simply raise their own children, rather than abandoning them to the mental disequilibrium in which today the reign of television consists (which, in our present world, tends to diminish everything that might be elevated, crushing and literally wiping out all other social organization of transmission and, of course, first of all, the family and the school), but this human being is always in an original relation, always fragile, but always renewing itself, to the question of his or her own elevation, and to the question of the elevation of his or her fellows – and, in particular, of his or her descendants, or his or her posterity.

In spite of this, each human being knows from experience, and immediately, and without any doubt, and hence *before* any experience, that within them lies that fatigue and that fragility that drags them down, beneath themselves, and beneath all of that which, before them, was conquered by his or her ancestors [*ascendants*], who then instilled in him or her their ascendancy [*qui conquirent ainsi sur lui leur ascendant*], that is, their authority. Each human being knows this, and that is why each man must combat himself, ceaselessly having to struggle against that which, in him, could lead him to no longer be himself, to no longer *ex-sist*. Hence the case of Richard Durn, that miserable human being who, no longer feeling that he ex-sisted, came to know that he was going to 'commit evil'. Because to be oneself, to ex-sist, to never be reduced to mere subsistence, is to be that which, in itself, raises itself up against *destructive tendencies – without which, however, no elevating force would be possible*. The life-drive, for example, is a tendency that constitutes itself as nothing other than what *composes* with the death-drive. Such is the *duplicity* of the motive of individuation, a duplicity that, *when psycho-social individuation enters into a phase of decomposition*, suddenly liberates – within those individuals who suffer the most and are the most fragile, those whose primordial narcissism has been destroyed – the worst expressions of mere instinct, that which one calls a transgression [*passer à l'acte*].

The process of psychic and collective individuation, precisely insofar as it ties together the *psyche* and the social, where the *psyche* is an originarily social reality, is in principle that which maintains this *psyche* as turned towards what surpasses it and stands above it: desire, insofar as desire is not merely crude instinct [*la pulsion brute*] but rather the *always already social* interaction of drives – insofar as this is the *composition of the death- and life-drives*, the play between which is translated *socially* as the *composition of the synchronic and the diachronic*.

Today, the capitalist process tends to engender the decomposition of these tendencies, rather than articulating them in a becoming-social of psychic becoming, which is just as much the becoming-psychic – that is, singular – of social becoming. Capitalism is a stage of Western psycho-social individuation, now planetarized, depending upon a technical becoming which has itself become planetary, and, more precisely, upon a *generalization of grammatization throughout technical becoming and throughout the entire world* (this is the becoming-mnemo-technological of the entire technical system). And given all this, what must immediately be added is that capitalism, as a process of individuation, a carrier of composing tendencies, has now reached a stage in which these tendencies tend on the contrary to oppose each other, and hence a stage in which capitalism itself decomposes.

I have tried to show, in 'To Love, to Love Me, to Love Us: From September 11 to April 21' (in *Acting Out*), that this decomposition principally resides in the tendency of capitalism to hyper-synchronize the temporalities of consciousnesses, to eliminate their diachronies and, as such, to annul their singularities by turning them into particularities, that is, *mere parts of a whole*. In this way, capitalism, in its hyper-industrial – that is, hyper-computational – stage, expresses a *totalitarian tendency* consisting in the tendency to reduce everything to calculation, to turn *all* singularity into mere *parts* of a whole. Capitalism thereby tends towards self-destruction – because it destroys credit as much as the *motives* of production (that is, a demotivation of work takes place) and of consumption [*consommer*] (that is, a consumptive wasting away [*consomption*] takes place, in the form of the disgust which the consumer comes to feel for himself).

It is this tendency of capitalism that it is a matter of combating. But this tendency, such as it finds expression today – that is, as a specific stage of the process of grammatization, its digital stage, making it possible to mobilize calculation technologies in order to control behaviour – does nothing other than bring to a planetary level a tendency that inhabits every *psyche*. It is thus a matter of *ensuring that this tendency recomposes with its counter-tendency within the new conditions opened up by the computational stage of grammatization*, and of ensuring that this recomposition is the invention of a process that socializes psychic tendencies, so that calculation leads to a new epoch of singularity.

Before getting to this question, however, which will constitute the content of the following chapters and of the second volume of this work, we must deepen our understanding of the consequences of the fact that, if the *psyche* were not itself already the bearer of a tendency which capitalism, decomposing the play of tendencies that form the social, liberates as a *base* tendency, the base tendency of capitalism itself, then none of this would have any more effect on psychic and social existence than pouring water on a duck's back. This social necrosis – *exploiting* the most base propensities rooted deeply within the *psyche*, and exploiting them in a sort of mechanical or automatic way, that is, *not intentionally*, but merely as the *extremization* of the unprecedented consequences of that process which capitalism is insofar as it is the *paradoxical* question of its *credit* – is at the origin of what I here call *mécréance*, that is, dis-belief or miscreance.

If there is a singular combat that today must be taken up, then taking up this combat requires the preliminary proposition that the necessity of combat would be permanent: existence is that which must struggle against its own decay (against that which I will analyse in a coming volume as its beastly stupidity [*bêtise*]), and society will always have been that which fights its *necessarily* base part – 'necessarily', since it consists in a *tendency which, when it composes with its counter-tendency, is also the source of the dynamism of society*. In other words, the process of individuation is a state of permanent war, but a war contained and transformed through psycho-social *competition* [*émulation*], which the Greeks called *eris* – the elevation towards an always possible best, *ariston*.

5. The worst and the best in the epoch of nihilism as questions of war and class struggle

But *eris* may always turn into destructive struggle, and become *discord*. The *ariston*, as a motive, is therefore duplicitous: the best may contain the worst. The inverse is also true, and this is why Nietzsche has Zarathustra say:

> man has need of that which is worst in him if he wishes to reach what is best.[13]

This 'worst' is the drive which, or, rather, the play of life- and death-drives which, when bound, form desire as individuation, but which, unbound, destroy all individuation.

In the Greek city, the *culture* of moderation or measurement [*la culture de la mesure*], of the *metron*, like piety, incessantly brings the citizenry to recall that their mortal situation, between beasts and gods, is ambiguous,[14] one that may always turn bad, where everything may always turn into its opposite, where what one wished to raise up suddenly breaks down and collapses.

> And when he has found happiness, he ruins it.
> His life is a strange and bitter divorce.[15]

This difference in the interior of the same, which constitutes the duplicity of the best and of the *eris* that aims towards it, is that which necessitates *sacrifice*: as the *recollection* of its ambiguous condition, Greek mortality, that is, Greek politics insofar as it is tragic, is a *culture* to the extent that it is a *cult* – it cultivates the *question* of that which, in the best, can become the worst, and, as such, it takes care of (cultivates) its individuation.

Now, taking care (*cura*) of individuation is necessitated by the fact that aiming towards the best is inscribed within *technicity*, which is the origin of this individuation process, and as its (de)fault of origin, but as a fault that is necessary [*un défaut qu'il faut*]. This is why Prometheus is the tragic god par excellence, as Deleuze too underlines in relation to Nietzsche,[16] and all Greek sacrificial practice is a recollection of the *conflict* between the Titans and the Olympians, between Prometheus and Zeus, which happens also to be the origin of mortals – as recounted by Hesiod at the end of the eighth century BCE, by Aeschylus at the beginning of the fifth century, and by Plato, through Protagoras, at the beginning of the fourth.

In other words, the *question of war* is inevitably contained within the *question of technics*: the technical tool is above all an organ of predation and defence. Technicity, as a system [*système*], constitutes the artificial and social system [*dispositif*] of predation and defence from the beginning of humanity. As such, all *ars* is the art of war. And yet, in this worst lies also the best: this art, this *tekhnè*, is also that which permits, and as

the *possibility* of *eris*, the trans-formation of the *struggle for life*
into a *socialization* establishing a peace. That is, also, into a super-
egoization,[17] which is a sublimation of the libidinal economy, and
which we refer to, with Valéry, as a spiritual economy.

All this, however, only arises as the result of a care, a cult, a
cure, a culture perpetually dedicated to this difference in the interior of the same. This is because the technical system bears within
it a *tension*, between predatory and defensive instruments on the
one hand, through which humanity makes war with itself, and
through which the individuation process may be ruined (hence the
Greek obsession with *stasis*, that is, civil war), and, on the other
hand, the potential contained by the technical system to open up
a socialization, insofar as it can open a space for peace *and trust*,
that trust which is indispensable to prosperity. As such, the technical system is the *ars*, as the condition through which are *articulated* and *disarticulated* the tendencies that are founded in the
drives and *eris* as *expression of desire*.

Socialization consists in a unifying synchronization that one can
always also analyse as domination and polemical (eristic) diachronization, wherein singularities are formed as the *sublimation* of
war – thus as the sublime expression of the worst becoming the
best. Such an analysis demands that we understand the question
of *logos* as at once the expression of the motive of a *one* and as
a *polemos* of the multiple singularities of the Presocratic Greeks,
but also, more generally, this analysis demands that we try to
understand the question of reason – and to understand it *anew*,
that is, as motive, mobility, design, and beyond *ratio*, on which
this question has run aground.

And it is also through this question of the technicity of existence that one must understand the Marxist questions of class
struggle and of the exploitation of man by man: Marx confirms
the irreducible character of war. But this irreducibility does not
mean a vocation for the worst: it must become the horizon of
something better, which Marx calls communism. For all that,
however, a great weakness of Marxist thought, a weakness
aggravated by the misunderstandings that have characterized
Marxism (when, for example, it confuses the proletariat with
the working class), has been that it has understood class struggle
as the possible and necessary *elimination* of one tendency of the

exteriorization process in which social life consists by another, contrary tendency. The Marxist thought of struggle then becomes *reactive* in the Nietzschean sense: it does not think tragically; there is within Marxism still something Christian (that is, for Nietzsche, Platonic), something that *does not want to think tragically, that is, to think through composition* rather than through opposition.

6. The technicity of existence, *ressentiment* and affirmation as combat

Class struggle appears from that point to constitute a modern figure of *ressentiment*, that is, a typical expression of what, for Nietzsche, it is a matter of overcoming: the epoch of nihilism.

Examining this crucial question is particularly delicate, in that it is notably entangled in a great confusion that still reigns in the reception of Nietzsche. This confusion has often, and very paradoxically, concealed the fact that Nietzsche's thought concerning nihilism is before anything else that of a *permanent combat* led *within* becoming, and that becoming, in its nihilistic epoch, is experienced by Nietzsche first of all as a *becoming-herdish*, that is, as a *mortal threat* brought about by the *adaptive injunction* and the levelling [*égalisation*] of all things against *exceptions* – that is, against singularities, insofar as these form horizons of the best.[18]

The ordeal of nihilism is *as such* that *massive weakness* that threatens force, and *where becoming is a becoming-weak*, a *becoming-base*, that is, the becoming-*hegemonic* of a tendency that tends to annul, *through its mass*, the tendency constituting it, that is, to annul its counter-tendency: nihilism is the name of this de-composition, and this is what the thought of affirmation *combats*. Nietzsche warns his readers: this growth of the desert shall last two centuries – 'What I relate is the history of the next two centuries.'[19] Henceforth, *to affirm* can only mean *to combat*. And this 'advent of nihilism' is that which, concretely expressing itself as the growth of the industrial world – that is, also, of the desert, and as the fulfilment [*accomplissement*] of the capitalist process, as the grammatization and installation of control societies – fails to redouble this concretization, that is, fails to overcome it through the invention of a new stage of the psychic and collective individuation process.

It is a caricature of Nietzsche's thought to turn it into a philosophy of *acquiescence to becoming in all its forms*, a *yes* to everything that one must endlessly repeat like a simpleton in the face of whatever happens to transpire. To affirm does not mean to acquiesce. If *weakness* is that which reacts against becoming-as-force, and if Nietzsche is the philosopher who speaks of the need to struggle *for* becoming, this is because weakness is a counter-force *in* becoming, which, oblivious to becoming, is what makes it possible to say that weakness is a counter-tendency, because *becoming is double*: there is in becoming a *becoming-spontaneous* which is a becoming-weak, an *automaton* that reacts against becoming-as-force, that is, against becoming-as-future – but that is also the *condition* of force.

Becoming-weak is that which wants *to change nothing in the levelling* of all things, and it will constitute, Nietzsche prophesies, 'the history of the next two centuries'. In short, this becoming-weak is what always says yes – like a simpleton. Insofar as it is that which does not want to change anything, becoming-weak is either *ressentiment* par excellence, or that which submits and says yes to the state of affairs that produces this resentment. Today, *ressentiment* is what is produced, and on a massive scale, by technical becoming. *What could face up to resentment?* This is a *political* question, to which any credible response must also have something to say about the following question: *what faces up to technics insofar as, having today become industrial, that is, technoscientific, it has become the principal source of* ressentiment? As for this second question, to which I will return, let us simply say for now that, firstly, one *must not say that one knows what must be done when one doesn't know*, and, secondly, that it is essential that *this not-knowing become an object of political attention*.

In other words, being political today, which always means before anything else constituting a political *thought*, and a thought that could only ever be a *collective intelligence*, that is, an intelligence that does not take those to whom it addresses itself to be simpletons, has the task before any other of publicly posing the question of the *effort* that must be made in a situation of not-knowing, and that constitutes the task of elaborating the psycho-social doubling up of that epochal redoubling that is automatically constituted by computational technology, insofar as it is the final epoch of grammatization characterizing Western individuation.

As for the first question (what could face up to *ressentiment?*), the essential thing here is to pose in principle that *in order to face up to* ressentiment *one must not cultivate* ressentiment, which is *difficult*, because *ressentiment* engenders resentment. This is one of *ressentiment's* most dangerous characteristics, so that, very often, those who try to oppose resentment sink, lamentably, into *ressentiment. Ressentiment* is this 'counter' that it is only possible to struggle against by affirming before any other consideration that the only way to encounter an adversary is to understand better than they do, if at all possible, their adversity – or, at least, to have some way of understanding one's adversary, however evil they may be.

Ressentiment is the nihilistic face of a combat that must be led *within* becoming, *with* it, but *in order to transform it into a future*. What makes it so difficult for us to understand this *and to do something about it*, we who are Nietzsche's heirs, and who find ourselves in the very heart of this nihilism that was promised for two centuries through his warning, is the fact that the worst lies within the best, and conversely – and, consequently, that becoming is *as such* a struggle, a combat. The larger question is, therefore: what must actually be combated, that is, what must one *do*, after one recognizes the scourge of *ressentiment?*

Nietzsche is a tragic thinker and his most powerful thought is that a tendency only exists as that which constitutes the *condition* of its counter-tendency, which it cannot therefore be a matter of eliminating. But it is just such a *drive for elimination* that, precisely, also characterizes *ressentiment* and, in particular, does so *insofar as it is founded on guilt*. Guilt is that which sees a *fault* [*faute*] where there is a flaw [*défaut*], and thus which does not want to understand that the flaw is *necessary* [*qu'il faut le défaut*]. The inheritors of the thinking of nihilism caricature its thinker when, under the pretext that it is necessary to say *yes* to becoming, and thus deluding themselves when they believe they escape *ressentiment* and guilt, they leap across two centuries by failing to see that *an historic struggle is underway and in full swing*. Such a *yes* to becoming is so impoverished that it turns precisely into its opposite, because it becomes, through haste, lazy thinking and a nihilistic *indigestion*, a *yes* to becoming-weak, a *yes* to becoming-herdish: it is the very denial of life, the victory of renunciation, that is, the victory of what, as far as Nietzsche was concerned, was the most base, and this is *one of the most frightening fulfilments* of the Nietzschean prophecy that one could imagine – the advent of nihilism laying hold of Nietzsche's thought itself in order to turn it into nothing more than the bleating of sheep.

Now, what characterizes the two centuries that for Nietzsche remained *still entirely to come*, that he *sees coming* in his present, from his epoch, is the fact that the second industrial revolution takes place, and that it does so as, precisely, the intensification of industrial becoming. Industrial becoming is what at once brings a *new* force, the promise of a future that, after the death of God, will break with two thousand years of Pauline Platonism and badly digested Christianity, but that *for now* takes the form of a becoming-herdish, that will be for a long time, for two centuries, the exhausting of this reign, *the reign of exhaustion* even, that is, of *discredit* – which means in the first place the death of God: a becoming-old, a *decadence*.

It is through the technical becoming that capitalism constitutes – as the pursuit of the industrial revolution – that this reign of exhaustion spreads, thereby increasing the desert. Nietzsche's thought is not the delirium of a philologist lost in his books and becoming mad, isolated in his visions: it is the interpretation of a world undergoing complete transformation, that of its industrialization, which will soon lead to the First World War, and it is an interpretation that calls for the fulfilment of this transformation, that is, a call to a combat of life against its nihilistic mortification. To interpret and to transform (all values) here *become* the same thing, change meaning, and are not opposed: this amounts to saying that they are *performative*. But the trans-formation in which interpretation as combat henceforth consists is preceded by transformation in the form of becoming-spontaneous, to which it is only possible to say *yes* while transforming this precisely through a performative (combative) interpretation of that which, in this spontaneity, also and automatically entails becoming-herdish.

In this *automatic* transformation of the world that is industrialization, technics is therefore and always the instrument of a struggle, of which war is the extreme version, but that also proceeds more stealthily and silently during peacetime, when nihilism tends, as becoming-herdish, to stifle its counter-tendency, that is, to *decompose* becoming. To fail to see this is to hypostasize this becoming, as if it were only a matter of a simple unity, that is, finally, as if becoming was merely the movement of being, was merely being in time. Now, what Nietzsche thinks under this name of becoming is a *process*, that process of *individuation* of which Simondon, in the twentieth century, takes up the torch.

In short, Marxist nihilism may wish to *oppose*, as class struggle, 'good' and 'bad' tendencies, it being a matter of eliminating the latter, but it is also true that the *reception* of Nietzsche *itself hypostasizes* becoming and makes it *return to being*: it deifies it, idolizes it, or *idealizes* it, as something good in itself. And in doing so it ignores the fact that, for Nietzsche more than for any other thinker, a force exists only in its relation to another force, and that becoming is always already divided. Becoming is intrinsically duplicitous [*duplice*], and its law is that of struggle. The *yes* is not acquiescent, and affirmation is not a 'letting be' that then turns into a *letting go*. To affirm is to *combat* – weakness, debasement, disbanding and renunciation of life.

The *theatre* of this individuation struggling *for and against itself* – for Nietzsche, as for Simondon in his analysis of becoming-proletarian as loss of individuation, and as for us who know the hyper-industrial age – is capitalism. Capitalism must go to the end of its process, and we remain utterly ignorant about the way this will turn out. On the other hand, we can describe this process and what, in it, threatens to brutally interrupt it. This process is the expression of becoming insofar as it is always duplicitous, that is, tragic – and what I here call combat is less the class struggle than it is the struggle between *tendencies*.

These are the *figures* – proper to the capitalist age, and to that epoch of capitalism that I call hyper-industrial – of what constitutes the *entire* process of psychic and collective individuation. But in the course of all that which, via capitalism, leads grammatization from its *mechanized* stage and into the digital and computational stage of control technologies, these tendencies play out to their extremes. And this *capitalist extremism*, manifested in all those extremisms *engendered by capitalism*, calls for a specific critique, one that presupposes a thought of technics, but one that would also be a critique of metaphysics on the grounds that it is a blockage rendering unthinkable the originary technicity of the individuation process.

7. Opposition, composition and decomposition in the play of the world

One of Nietzsche's most valuable contributions to the critique of metaphysics was his genealogy of guilt, insofar as guilt is a metaphysics that breaks with the tragic spirit by always and everywhere seeking the guilty, by *opposing* good and evil. It is necessary, in combat, for adversaries to *oppose* one another, but each of these adversaries is the representative [*porte-parole*], for their side, of a tendency that it cannot be a matter of eliminating, yet with which one must struggle. And adversaries represent, through their struggle, what Nietzsche himself called *eris*, or 'good discord', which is indeed an opposition, but which is also the way in which those tendencies represented by these adversaries com-pose a process, posing together, and one against the other, that process of which combat would be only a part, or rather, a *stage*: a stage of an individuation. Opposition, as the play of forces, plays out a more elementary composition, involving what Simondon called the *phase difference* [*déphasage*] inherent to the process of individuation, and it is for this reason that it cannot be a matter of seeking in the adversary an enemy who would be the *cause* of evil, or evil itself: the enemy is only the representative, the support or the vector of a tendency – it is a *phase* of a course, of a current which is in essence multiphase, just as the flow of a river is comprised of eddies that produce the current and that, as such, determine its course. That the force represented by an adversary *tends* to make itself hegemonic is inevitable: the force that the adversary represents dominates it, and the adversary defends it with the certainty of being right. And the adversary has, in fact, their reasons, their motives: the adversary, too, moves by design.

The critique of the process, and of a stage of the process, does not consist, therefore, in condemning the guilty, but in analysing the limits of the process, those limits which mean that while it is possible for a tendency to effectively become hegemonic, this would also mean it becomes *self*-destructive, or, as Jacques Derrida puts it, auto-immune:[20] the temptation always remains, *on both sides* of any adversity over which a struggle occurs, to purely and simply eliminate the adversary, but this could only consist in eliminating oneself, given that combat can only take place *and be pursued* to the degree that it permits the continuation [*se pour-suivre*] of the play of forces. Now, these are the *stakes: that combat continues.* The stakes involved here are whether this combat is able to resume: combat is a game. And the stakes of this game are the *elevation* of adversaries from their opposition, an opposition which masks a more profound composition, and which is the pursuit of individuation operating through every party within the game, and a pursuit that is therefore never reduc-ible, in its essence, to a single party.

In this case, the play of forces without doubt refers to a game that is singularly complex: it is the *play of the world* as a process of psychic and collective individuation, in which the composition of tendencies is the effect of this tension lying within life itself, of this *inadequation* within life, and of this phase difference engen-dered by technicity. That is to say, this is the role played by the trace, by 'death' that 'seizes life', that heritage genealogically accumulated in the form of what I have called *epiphylogenesis*, the mnemo-technical *capitalization* of the experience of ascen-dants in the life of descendants, and where it must be understood that this epiphylogenesis does not cease transforming itself. This is what is constituted as a technical system, and this is itself an element of a process of individuation, that individuates *itself too* within the play of forces. It is in this way that the play of the world is singularly complex: within it, *more than two* forces play themselves out.

Now, the individuation of the technical system constitutes a third system, and this is what does not cease to *change the rules of the play of forces*. The rules of the play of the world ceaselessly find themselves challenged and, as such, produce epochs and *regu-larly* become *outdated* [*révolues*]. Such is the play of *permanent revolution*, that is, of the *eternal return of the same stake: to raise itself*, to go further in the composition of forces, so that, within that process of individuation that is becoming, a future for this process can be discovered, the possibility of the continuation of the process through the invention of singularities, which are the incalculable projections of the opening of this play, the opening of that which, in itself, plays itself out as the indetermination of the future, the improbability of the future as the worst and the best. Such is *eris*.

The constant of this game is the technicity of existence: from *Homo erectus* until ourselves, passing through Lascaux, the *composition of technics with life* that we are, as composition of death and life, *constitutes* this process of *constant* transformation that is psycho-social individuation,[21] insofar as the doubly *epokhal* redoubling of technics is the *pursuit* of life by means other than life. The technicity of existence is the constant of which the variables are the ways that this composition translates itself into systems of technical organs, into social organizations, and into psychic organizations.[22] In the West, these ways are expressed in pairs which can be seen as oppositions, but which are always more profoundly compositions: mortal/immortal (the tragic age), soul/body (Christianity), capital/labour (capitalism).

Today, however, it is the very possibility of the *continuation* of the game which makes us question, and which is called into question. And there is no doubt that this fact is posed before us with the force of *terrifying evidence*. While technical power exceeds all measure, so too the expressions of the death-drive and the renunciations of life multiply themselves, to the point that life has become herdish nihilism, self-destructive transgression [*passages à l'acte*], *or stupefied if not stupid passivity* – that is, *resigned impotence*. Thus plays out the *decomposition* of forces – 'thus', that is, through grammatization as the computational control of behaviour, the hyper-synchronization of psychic individualities, and through psycho-social disindividuation, as individualities in general, the *I* and the *we* that we are, disindividuate themselves in becoming the *they* of the herd which consumes. This consumption [*consommation*] is a *consumption* [*consomption*] of individualities, notably in the industrial democracies: no longer projecting any possibility of pursuing individuation, either psychically or collectively, they no longer believe anything, no longer want anything, and can no longer do anything.

This moment, which is the height of the decadence in which nihilism consists, fully accomplishes, for the totality of existence, and beyond subsistence, that loss of individuation that initially took the form, as mechanization, of the proletarianization of the worker. This moment reveals the reality lying behind what until recently was still called progress, that is, it reveals the inversion [*renversement*] of all belief and, therefore, of all belief in progress itself. Hence this progress, in turn, shows itself to be self-destructive. What had been presented either as belief in the worker insofar as proletarian force became revolutionary, or else as belief in capital insofar as this referred to the spread of market exchange and the correlative extension of consumption within democracy, now appears to be the consumption [*consommation*] of democracy by itself, its consumption [*consomption*].

This collapse in the belief in progress reveals an immense political miscreance and disbelief and a catastrophic discredit for democracy, all of which does not fail to affect major capitalist enterprises themselves, given that it occurs at the same time as all those scandals involving Enron, Vivendi, Parmalat, Andersen Consulting, and so on. It is the *spirit of capitalism* which thereby crumbles.

8. The aporia of capitalism

The collapse of the belief in politics has a history intrinsically tied to capitalism, to the industrial revolution, and to the fall of onto-theologico-political metaphysics. This history is tied, in other words: (1) to the separation of capital and labour; (2) to mechanization insofar as it permits this separation to spread (this is the proletarianization of producers); and (3) to the reconciliation of science and technics, which becomes technoscience and permanent innovation. The end of onto-theology as the discourse on being, which is also the end of theologico-political individuation, occurs when science begins to explore the possibilities of becoming, in becoming techno-logy and permanent innovation under the pressure of capital investment, or, in other words, according to *selections from among possibilities*, selections determined according to the imperatives of development, that is, submitted to the hegemony of subsistence criteria. That is what Hegel, Marx, Nietzsche

and Freud analysed, each in their own way, as the death of
God. This becoming, that presents itself in the first place as progress, separates capital and labour by investing in machinery,
enabling the formalization and exteriorization of the processes of
production, that is, the grammatization of the production process,
and, thereby, the massification of labour and the reduction of
production costs. This is how the figure of the proletarian comes
to be drawn.

As I have frequently recalled, Simondon analyses the proletarianization of work as a loss of individuation, where the worker,
who was once the *technical individual*, becomes the servant of the
tool-bearing machine, which becomes the *new* technical individual. Thus the reality of proletarianization is, more than pauperization, the worker's *loss of knowledge*, the worker tending to become
unskilled *pure labour force* – and lacking any *motive* to work
beyond the need to subsist. In this way, the worker [*ouvrier*]
becomes a proletarian, which also means that the proletarian
ceases to be a worker [*ouvrier*]: the industrial revolution transforms the *workers of the world* [*ouvreurs de monde*] into proletar-
ians, those who had been, in their way, workers insofar as they
operated with their *work*-hands [*mains d'*oeuvres – manual
labour], labourers [*travailleurs*] and producers of *work* in general.[23]

In the twentieth century, however, mnemo-technologies supporting the culture and programme industries, mnemo-technologies
that were initially analogical and are today digital, and that took
the form of information and communication technologies, were
implemented on a massive scale, thereby constituting a new stage
of grammatization, and as such a new age of capitalism. This is
how the globalization of capitalism was completed, by imposing
the *proletarianization of the consumer* – after the earlier separation of the producer and the consumer that resulted from mechanization. And consumers, in turn, find themselves disindividuated:
just as workers-become-proletarian find themselves deprived of
the capacity to work the world through their work, that is, through
their *savoir-faire*, so too *consumers lose their savoir-vivre* insofar
as this means their singular way of being in the world, that is, of
existing.

It is in this way that the total proletarian emerges, expropriated
of all knowledge, condemned to a life-without-knowledge, that is,

without savours [*saveurs*], thrown into an insipid and, at times, squalid [*immonde*] world: at the same time economically, symbolically and libidinally immiserated. Just as the proletarianization of the worker is the *rationalization of subsistence* such that it ends in a *pure becoming-commodity* of labour force, that is, of the body, so too the proletarianization of consumers is the *rationalization of existence* as the *becoming-commodity of consciousness*, which is to say, as well, the reduction of consumers to subsistence conditions and the annihilation of their existence: this is what the Le Lay affair demonstrates. It is a matter of controlling the behaviour of bodies insofar as they consume and in order that they consume, and, as such, the times of consciousness become audiences constituting a new commodity. Obviously consciousnesses do not sell *themselves* on the market of conscious-time: that is done by *brokers* in *buying power* who furnish to investors access to these consciousnesses, in order that they may conform to behavioural standards permitting the *reduction of the diversity of existences to calculable and therefore manageable particularities of a set of customers*, segmented by niche marketing.

The proletarianization of consumption is the response of the capitalist process to the tendency, induced by productivity gains, for the rate of profit to decline: capital henceforth increases its profit margins mainly by extending its markets, which becomes the motor of planetarization, as units of production become delocalized. This means an ever-increasing circulation and deterritorialization, concretized through the intermediary of digitalization and the convergence of information and communication technologies, constituting a *planetary grammatization of behaviour, of production as well as consumption*, that is, a planetary disexistentialization of the gestures of work or, in other words, a *planetary loss of savoir-faire*, and constituting as well a particularization of existence inducing a *planetary loss of savoir-vivre*, that is, a planetary loss of individuation, a generalization of the process of proletarianization to all modes of existence and subsistence.

This is also the implementation of a planetary process of adoption, driven by the capturing, harnessing and rational channelling of libido. Now, there is also a *tendency for libidinal energy to decline*: a liquidation of singularity (of *savoir-faire* and *savoir-vivre*) that *contradicts* the constitution of desire. But this is not simply a new example of the 'contradictions' of capitalism. It involves an *aporia* lying within hyper-industrial capitalism itself, insofar as the question is no longer only economic: it is the spirit of capitalism, and its rationality, that is, its reason, that here encounters its own limits insofar as it becomes self-destructive. Reason, understood by the spirit of capitalism as *ratio* and rationalization, that is, as reckoning [*comput*] and rational accounting [*comptabilité rationnelle*] (as shown, notably, by Weber), tends to destroy the *motives* for producing as well as consuming. Such is the *catastrophe* of the industrial democracies, at the end of a long history of training [*dressage*], a long history of attempts to incite increased labour and then to incite increased consumption. Weber described the earliest forms of such attempts, taking place at the origins of pre-industrial capitalism and through-out the course of the eighteenth century, yet Weber never managed to grasp the question of consumption. Nor did Marx, whose causal models Weber nevertheless contests, by opening the question of a spirit defined as trust, and where trust is understood as calculation.

9. 'Remember, that credit is money.' The spirit of capitalism as the calculability of service to God and the measurability of occupied time (or *negotium*), or, the birth of capitalism as the accountability of time

In order to develop his analysis of the constitution of the *spirit* of capitalism as *Beruf*, that is, as both profession in the sense of a profession of faith, and as 'vocation for making money' ('the capitalistic system so needs this devotion to the calling of making money'[24]), Weber recalls that workers, as soon as their salaries increase, work less – they prefer to take their time:[25]

> A man does not 'by nature' wish to earn more and more money, but simply to live as he is accustomed to live and to earn as much as is necessary for that purpose.[26]

If one cannot strictly say that the worker who *works* [*ouvre*] is, through his work, directly *turned* towards his free and social time (what had, in an earlier age, been called *otium*), then we can nevertheless at least say that such a worker is *predisposed* to do so, that he is predisposed to grab hold of time on the grounds that it is *his* time, and to do so insofar as, although he is a producer dedicated to subsistence, he is *also* someone who *exists*. Work must not be opposed here to rest: they must be distinguished, but in order to understand in what way they are composed, to understand the way in which work can echo what is given in rest, that is, outside the cares solely of subsisting – even if Weber's examples are very diverse: the situation of day labourers who sell their labour force each morning for the harvest is very different from that of the weavers who work to order and who are able to work from their own homes.

This time of existence is a gift of time when, in *otium*, as care, *cura*, it consists in *practices free of all the worries of subsistence*, free of all *negotium*. The worker certainly does not belong to the sphere of clerics who, alone, have the *privilege* of acceding properly to *otium*, in that they are in principle emancipated from the necessity of the *needy* (those needy alienated by and in *negotium*), that is, from the preoccupation with need – *negotium*, which, as *ethos* of capitalism, becomes on the contrary the *vocation* (*Beruf*) for business, the business of subsistence as model of life. But the worker, yet to be totally proletarianized and pauperized, even though he is indeed alienated by his obsession with need, nevertheless *participates* in the sphere of *otium* (and does so *insofar as he believes*) when he submits himself to the rituals of that cult of which the clerics are in charge.

Now, Weber shows how capitalism, in its pre-industrial phase and as the 'spirit' issuing from the Reformation, and therefore as a mutation of Christianity – a mutation in which one cannot ignore the context constituted by the advent of printing, which is therefore also the advent of a new era of grammatization[27] – is that which leads from the question of *belief*, wholly inscribed within a tradition, to that of *trust* [*confiance*], a trust *required* by what then appears, which is the process of *innovation*, and such that it presupposes a *rupture* with tradition, precisely insofar as it is the legacy of belief. Innovation may indeed characterize capitalism, Weber says, but the spirit of this capitalism does not amount to the lure of gaining a reward, but rather to the vocation of making money in order to facilitate the development of business – that is, *negotium* – to the point of extending its imperatives to every dimension of existence: to the point of annulling this existence itself. But this extremity will only be reached much later, *after Weber himself*, when the culture and programming industries pursue and extend the movement described by the spirit of capitalism, causing it to mutate – Weber, having no experience of the culture industry, is as unaware of this as Freud will be in his turn.[28]

Capitalism is therefore before anything else a new state of mind [*état d'esprit*] about business, leading to a mutation of the question of belief in the Western process of psycho-social individuation, the conditions of which capitalism thus redefines. According to Weber, this new *state of mind* comes from a turning point in Christian thought, Protestantism, that itself constitutes a transformation of belief and of the modalities of its expression, of its practice and of its individuation within the circle of the faithful. But with capitalism, this mutation in religious *spirit* leads to a rationalization that, itself, eventually clashes with this religious spirit *as belief*.

Benjamin Franklin, the official printer for the state of Pennsylvania, and whose father was a Calvinist, was for Weber the ideal type constituting the face of that new spirit that formed as capitalism emerged from its pre-industrial phase. Weber analyses various texts, called 'sermons', the earliest of which date from 1732. The Calvinist heritage consists in the doctrine that believes in the fulfilment of one's duty through worldly business [*affaires temporelles*] (in *negotium*), and such is already the spirit of the Reformation that, advocating 'asceticism in the world', denies in principle all difference between *otium* and *negotium*. This is translated by Franklin into the first commandment that time is money – which means first of all that service to God becomes *calculable* and *rational in this sense*: one can establish *ratios*, according to the sense in which accountants use this word.

Belief is transformed into *credit* obtained through trust insofar as it is itself calculable and *measures occupied time* (*negotium*):

> Remember, that *time* is money. He that can earn ten shillings a day
> by his labour, and goes abroad, or sits idle, one half of that day,

though he spends but sixpence during his diversion or idleness, ought not to reckon *that* the only expense; he has really spent, or rather thrown away, five shillings besides.

Remember, that *credit* is money.

It is, indeed, very much a matter of accounting: time becomes entirely accountable; and belief must become a credit such that it constitutes a *relation* [*rapport*], but a relation that *brings in* [*rapporte*], that is, that makes money proliferate as

> ... that which amounts to a considerable sum where a man has good and large credit, and makes good use of it.[29]

This amounts to a very profound transformation of motivation, that is, of reason: motivation as *Beruf*, profession (in the old sense of the word) or vocation, essentially translatable and measurable in terms of pecuniary gain, and as a consequence *essentially calculable*. It involves, as well, a new system of value where everything is equalized by the general equivalence that is money insofar as it is the possibility of reckoning without end [*comput sans reste*], *without exception*, and that prepares what Nietzsche will call the advent of nihilism:[30]

> He that kills a breeding-sow, destroys all her offspring to the thousandth generation. He that murders a crown, destroys all that it might have produced, even scores of pounds.[31]

Here, idleness is denounced as that through which time, escaping from business, is irremediably lost. Nothing can any longer escape *negotium*. This is how the culture industries extend functional efficacy to 'leisure' itself, by proletarianizing extra-productive existence, and by inventing, at the beginning of the twentieth century, and in the United States, the figure of the consumer. In the eighteenth century, however, and as Franklin explains, the spread of the imperatives of *negotium* in the new *ethos* evaluated friendship as a new sociability where trust became the *calculable bond* that substituted itself, at least in the world of entrepreneurs, for belief:

He that is known to pay punctually and exactly to the time
he promises, may at any time, and on any occasion, raise all the
money his friends can spare. The one who is known to pay punctually and exactly on the promised date, can at any moment and in
any circumstance procure money for himself that his friends have
saved [. . .] never keep borrowed money an hour beyond the time
you promised, lest a disappointment shut up your friend's purse
for ever.[32]

It is not here simply a matter of 'business sense', but rather, Weber
emphasizes, of an *ethic*, and:

The infraction of its rules is treated not as foolishness but as for-
getfulness of duty. That is the essence of the matter.[33]

The circumstance that he ascribes his recognition of the utility of
virtue to a divine revelation, which was intended to lead him in the
path of righteousness, shows that something more than mere gar-
nishing for purely egocentric motives is involved.[34]

And this is also the appearance of a new figure of the will to power,
a figure who takes

acquisition as the ultimate purpose of his life. Economic acquisition
is no longer subordinated to man as the means for the satisfaction
of his material needs.[35]

Nevertheless, as we have already seen, it is not man's nature to
seek to make money. It will therefore be, rather, a matter of training in this new vocation, this new *Beruf*.

Labour must, on the contrary, be performed as if it were an absolute end in itself, a vocation (*Beruf*). But such a state of mind is by
no means a product of nature [. . .] but can only be the product of
a long and arduous process of education.[36]

One of the pathways of this training is pauperization:

Another obvious possibility, to return to our example, since the
appeal to the acquisitive instinct through higher wage-rates failed,
would have been to try the opposite policy, to force the worker by

reduction of his wage-rates to work harder to earn the same amount that he did before.[37]

Don't people only work because and so long as they are poor?[38]

But the real question lies elsewhere: it is principally a matter of substituting for a way of life inherited from tradition *a new process of adoption* resting on the organization of society around the spirit of enterprise, such that it will never cease innovating, first of all through the organization of the relation between production and customer, and, much later (but Weber does not analyse this period, even though he evokes it in the introduction[39]), through the development of technology and mechanization. Now, it is with this question of innovation, and of the permanent transformation of social relations that it constitutes, *that trust is configured insofar as it is substituted for belief.*

10. The institution of 'absolute trust' in innovation as the liquidation of belief

Weber compares the spirit of an industrialist – who employs home-workers and who therefore seems to be a capitalist to the extent that his capital is invested in the work of others – with the new kind of entrepreneur who bears that spirit which alone characterizes capitalism. In the first case:

> The *form* of organization was in every respect capitalistic; the entrepreneur's activity was of a purely business character; the use of capital, turned over in the business, was indispensable; and finally, the objective aspect of the economic process, the book-keeping, was rational. But it was traditionalistic business, if one considers the *spirit* which animated the entrepreneur: the traditional manner of life, the traditional rate of profit, the traditional amount of work, the traditional manner of regulating the relationships with labour, and the essentially traditional circle of customers and the manner of attracting new ones. All these dominated the conduct of the business, were at the basis, one may say, of the *ethos* of this group of business men.
>
> Now at some time this leisureliness was suddenly destroyed, and often entirely without any essential change in the form of organization, such as the transition to a unified factory, to mechanized

weaving, etc. What happened was, on the contrary, often no more than this: some young man from one of the putting-out families went out into the country, carefully chose weavers for his employ, greatly increased the rigour of his supervision of their work, and thus turned them from peasants into labourers. On the other hand, he would begin to change his marketing methods by so far as possible going directly to the final consumer, would take the details into his own hands, would personally solicit customers, visiting them every year, and above all would adapt the quality of the product to their needs and wishes. At the same time he began to introduce the principle of low prices and large turnover. There was repeated what everywhere and always is the result of such a process of rationalization: those who would not follow suit had to go out of business. The idyllic state collapsed under the pressure of a bitter competitive struggle, respectable fortunes were made, and not let out at interest, but always reinvested in the business.[40]

The new question of trust – such that it is no longer simply faith, cultivated and maintained by tradition, but a mutual *engagement* [*fiance*] – a trust in this sense, which results in an 'ethic', that is, a behaviour submitted to rules of which the efficacy is calculable, as Franklin's sermons already indicate, is the result of this 'new state of mind': the goal of this new spirit is to engender an absolute trust in the innovations of capitalism, in *capitalism as the spirit of innovation*. This young entrepreneur forming the ideal type at the origin of capitalism must:

> command the absolutely indispensable confidence of his customers and workmen. [. . .] But these are ethical qualities of quite a differ-ent sort from those adapted to the traditionalism of the past.[41]

Capitalism is an innovation in the modes of production and consumption that must develop counter to tradition, since it requires the development of a trust that comes to collide with belief, and that as such constitutes a sort of *Aufklärung*. Insofar as tradition does not move, what maintains this immobility is belief, that very belief that is in the end destroyed by the trust sought by Weber's young entrepreneur. For:

these innovators [. . .] grown up in the hard school of life, calculating and daring at the same time, above all temperate and reliable,
shrewd and completely devoted to their business, [. . .] the ability
to free oneself from the common tradition, a sort of liberal
Aufklärung, seems likely to be the most suitable basis for such a
man's business success.[42]

In short, the *Aufklärung* inherited from philosophy is concretely
expressed as an ethics of calculation, and this amounts to a
destruction of belief through the calculation of trust, something
that can also be seen in Franklin's new concept of *friendship as
credit and amortization of existence*. This concept of friendship
depends upon the representation to oneself of an ego ideal, which
constitutes this as an epoch of the will to power, such that it will
become the norm that super-egos are constituted through *Beruf*,
and such that this constitutes a motive to live, a *raison d'être*, a
social rationality:

> If you ask them what is the meaning of their restless activity, why
> they are never satisfied with what they have, thus appearing so
> senseless to any purely worldly view of life, they would perhaps
> give the answer [. . .] that business with its continuous work has
> become a necessary part of their existence.[43]

These innovators as such resemble the consumer whose existence is destroyed by consumption and who, in order to compensate for that lack which consumes this existence, is incited to
consume more and more – there is an addiction to this new form
of will to power, which forms the origin of nihilism. Because, as
Weber himself notes, even though he certainly does not lack admir-
ation for these 'innovators', this is:

> in fact the only possible motivation, but it at the same time expresses
> what is, seen from the view-point of personal happiness, so irra-
> tional about this sort of life, where a man exists for the sake of his
> business, instead of the reverse.[44]

Now, this irrationality can be dissimulated so long as this other
motor of belief functions, according to which economic expansion

is social *progress*. But given that this expansion must submit production and consumption to the same logic of calculation, in the
sense of a levelling [*égalisation*] that wears down all possible
motives other than those that are addictive, it inevitably falls into
economic and political decadence: the decadence of the democracies, insofar as they implement an obsolete industrial model. And
this decadence lies particularly in the fact that this is a model that
severely thwarts human spirit, the spirit of human beings who
exist and are not content merely to subsist. And this thwarting of
spirit begins at the very moment when the capitalist 'innovator'
ushers forth a new spirit consisting in the replacement of existence
by subsistence at every level of society – a replacement that will
only be fully realized in the twentieth century, when the culture
industries succeed in creating generalized proletarianization. Now,
this liquidation of existence leads, precisely, to the opposite of the
intended goal (which is to create trust): this period is in fact characterized by mistrust, a mistrust induced as much by industrial
products, and in particular recent innovations, as by the generalized insecurity and discredit that increasingly and in advance
mortgages the business world, that is, *negotium*, as much as it
does political representation.

  This evolution is intrinsic to that new spirit which is nascent
capitalism, the application of calculability to every mode of existence, an evolution that progressively and completely rearranges
'our political, legal and economic institutions [. . .] purely as a
result of adaptation',[45] and that constitutes a struggle for survival
practically incompatible with all religious belief – but also, more
generally, with raising [*élévation*] insofar as it is an aim and a
practice which *desires the incalculability* of the one who raises, of
the ancestor [*ascendant*] and of his authority:

> The capitalistic system so needs this devotion to the vocation
> (*Beruf*) of making money, it is an attitude toward material goods
> which is so well suited to that system, so intimately bound up with
> the conditions of survival in the economic struggle for existence,
> that there can to-day no longer be any question of a necessary
> connection of that acquisitive manner of life with any single
> *Weltanschauung*. In fact, it no longer needs the support of any
> religious forces, and feels the attempts of religion to influence eco-

nomic life, insofar as they can still be felt at all, to be as much an unjustified interference as its regulation by the State. In such circumstances men's commercial and social interests do tend to determine their opinions and attitudes. Whoever does not adapt his manner of life to the conditions of capitalistic success must go under, or at least cannot rise.[46]

How could this activity, that was previously only the *poor side* of an existence the vocation of which was constituted in *otium*, how could this necessary side of the life of the needy, those whose *otium* also needed *negotium*, but who nevertheless had not hitherto constituted this *negotium* as the reason of their existence (that is, of existence as such, its 'sense'), how could this *negotium* come to be reconstituted such that *Beruf* is formed into an ethic, 'how could this activity, [until then] *at best tolerated by morality*, transform itself into a vocation in the sense of Benjamin Franklin?'[47]

It is doubtless not a matter, as Weber emphasizes, of considering what happened 'in the backwoods of Pennsylvania' as a simple reflection in the superstructure of a mutation in the infrastructure. It is a matter of a spiritual mutation that is not a consequence but on the contrary a cause of the appearance of capitalism, and that will enable the so-called 'infrastructure' characteristic of industrial capitalism to appear. What Luther brought into play was the *liquidation of that difference and hierarchy* that, hitherto, had constituted *negotium* insofar as it was defined as that which was not *otium*. It is doubtless Calvinism more than Lutheranism that concretizes this new spirit, but the initial condition of this spirit of capitalism derives from Luther's condemnation of monasticism, from that Luther for whom the evangelical counsels of monastic life, that is, the turning of the practices of *otium* into religious practice, are:

'dictated by the devil.' The monastic life is not only quite devoid of value as a means of justification before God, but he also looks upon its renunciation of the duties of this world as the product of selfishness, withdrawing from temporal obligations.[48]

It might be thought that this transformation seems relatively minor compared with the evolution of industrial mechanization and technology, and such a thought would be both correct and incorrect. It would be correct to conclude, as does Weber, that it is not a matter of a transformation of the means of production, of machines, of the 'infrastructure'; nor thus of proletarianization, even if, as we have seen, it is already a matter of pauperization. On the contrary, this ethic of *negotium* is tied both to *accounting* and to the *printing of the Bible*, making it accessible to all. Weber does not doubt that the Reformation is as such tied to a state of grammatization: printing, which constitutes, according to Sylvain Auroux, the 'second technological revolution'. And he does not doubt that this new epoch of grammatization constitutes a new retentional system that will soon be incorporated into the Protestant Church, and that amounts to a new regime in relation to *hypomnemata*. And if this is a matter of regimes of *hypomnemata*, then we must also recall that it is Michel Foucault who demonstrates the way in which, throughout the Epicurean and Stoic Roman epochs, and from the dawn of Christianity, the question of *otium* is constituted *precisely as monasticism*.

11.   From the art of living, *tekhnè tou biou*, to accounting expertise: *hypomnemata* as technologies of 'governing the self and others'

An original example of this monasticism:

> the *Vita Antonii* of Athanasius presents the written notation of actions and thoughts as an indispensable element of the ascetic life.[49]

This question of asceticism and of its techniques is very old, and it was for a long time considered *indispensable to the acquisition of the art of living*. But this question progressively becomes that of the practice of writing, the *practice of an hypomnesis*, that is, in the language of Plato, of an artificial memory, and here, contrary to what the *Phaedrus* recommends, it is therefore *hypomnesis* that supports a form of anamnesis,[50] the *anamnesis of self*:

> No technique, no professional skill, can be acquired without exercise; nor can the art of living, *tekhnè tou biou*, be learned without

an *askesis* that should be understood as a training of the self by oneself. This was one of the traditional principles to which the Pythagoreans, the Socratics, the Cynics had long attached a great importance. It seems that, among all the forms taken by this training (which included abstinences, memorizations, examinations of conscience, meditations, silence, and listening to others), writing – the act of writing for oneself and for others – came, rather late, to play a considerable role.[51]

The hypomnesis that for Plato orthographic writing constitutes[52] is a particular type of what I call *tertiary retention*. This particular type arises out of mnemo-techniques that appear in the wake of Neolithic sedentarization, sedentarization leading to the accumulation of surpluses, surpluses of which it was necessary to keep count, and this inaugurates the process of grammatization[53] through which the first forms of writing emerge. *Grammatization is in general the production of tertiary retentions* permitting symbolic fluxes and flows to be discretized and deposited, that is, permitting the spatialization of their temporality, notably in orthothetic forms, that is, permitting the re-accessing of engrammed fluxes without loss of content, and constituting therefore a surety and security of the archive, that is, also, a *belief* in the archive, which then supports the *arkhè*, that principle of hypomnesic practice that aims at maintenance and care and, as such, the cult. In this regard, the religions of the Book are such practices brought to the social level, and these religious practices have a history, of which the advent of Luther would constitute one crucial moment.

The discretization of fluxes in which grammatization consists as a weaving of tertiary retentions is always also inevitably the invention of new fluxes, and the transformation of the temporality of engrammed fluxes. It is in this way that the technique of the self that hypomnesis constitutes can, as practice, *transform* the self. It is also in this way that printing affects religious practice to the point of engendering a new Church, Protestantism.

The question of *hypomnemata*, to again take up Foucault's orthography, and such as he introduces it here in relation to monastic practice during the epoch of primitive Christianity, and thus as the support of the very thing condemned by Luther, for whom these practices are 'dictated by the Devil' insofar as they support a cult of *otium*, that is, a culture of distance and difference in relation to *negotium* – this question of *hypomnemata*, which raises the much broader question of tertiary retention in general, must be inscribed within the question of *technologies of power* studied by Foucault, and this inscription is necessary, despite the fact that Foucault did not himself succeed in explicitly doing so.

This is, indeed, here a matter of *technologies of the self*, that is, a subjectivation (which is a Foucauldian name for individuation) that is constituted, precisely, *outside* technologies of power. Now, the technology of *hypomnemata* is precisely *also* that of power insofar as writing founds law, a law that is public and criticizable, and as such political, and founds as well a difference between fact and law – but it also founds, and much earlier, accountability. Foucault thus emphasized the importance of writing, but he questioned neither the Platonic discourse on *hypomnesis* and the philosophical and metaphysical occultation to which it gives rise, nor the ortho-graphic constitutivity of the *polis*, that is, the role of grammatization in the process of *psychic and collective* individuation giving birth to the West.

On the other hand, Foucault did emphasize that practices of *hypomnemata* extend far beyond the ascetic context and the 'cultivated' public:

> *Hupomnemata*, in the technical sense, could be account books, public registers, or individual notebooks serving as memory aids. Their use as books of life, as guides for conduct, seems to have become a common thing for a whole cultivated public.[54]

'Cultivated' here means living within the practice of *otium*, this practice being precisely that of these *hypomnemata*. The *hypomnemata*:

> constituted a material record of things read, heard, or thought.[55]

In brief, the ascetic practice of *hypomnemata* involves mnemotechnics and is, in this sense, a technology. Now, as orthographic hypomnesis, this also constitutes social and political power properly speaking – that is, *precisely, as that power that is, first of all, juridical* (in particular, that profane power of the judge about which Hesiod complains to the goddess Dike, because this written justice harmed him, just as that of Creon will damage Antigone and Polynices) – but which becomes, later, that technology *demanding* [*revendiquée*] that one maintain an *individual* power over oneself, the technology of philosophical, then religious, asceticism, that is, also, the technology of a power to psychically individuate oneself. (And here, one must insist on the fact that hypomnesis is *already* a power, a power that has *not been claimed* [*non revendiqué*] and has even been *occluded* by all that thinking which constitutes itself as philosophical, and which is in truth a stage and a significant modality of Western individuation: it is essential to it. This is what I have attempted to show numerous times, but in particular in 'How I Became a Philosopher'.[56])

In other words, *hypomnemata* are technologies of individuation, such that individuation is psychic and collective, that is, social and political.

In an address delivered in Brazil in 1976, Foucault emphasized the fact that *juridicism*, in terms of a theory of power, implied the idea that power rests on the exercise of interdiction, of the limit, constituting a conception of power as restrictive – something Marx had already denied in Book II of *Capital*. This is the idea of power from which Foucauldian thought understood itself to be, precisely, emancipating itself, and to be doing so by analysing power throughout the range of its technologies:

> [O]ne could better develop an analysis of power that would not simply be a negative juridical conception of power, but a conception of a technology of power.[57]

> [T]he West never had a system for the representation, the formulation and the analysis of power other than law and the system of law. And I believe that this is the reason for which, when it comes down to it, we have not had, until recently, other possibilities of analysing power besides utilizing these elementary, fundamental, etc., notions that are those of law, of rules, of the sovereign, of the delegation of power, etc. I believe that it is this juridical conception of power, this conception of power derived from law and the sovereign, from rule and prohibition, of which we must now rid ourselves if we want to proceed to an analysis not just of the representation of power but of the real functioning of power.[58]

For all that, what constitutes the real functioning of juridical power, as well as all the other forms of power, are technologie*s*.

We have just seen, however, that in the ascetic practice of *hypomnemata as well as* with *juridico-political* technology, it is a matter of an individuation: whether within the city, or outside it. What this means is that, even from the point of view of the 'juridical conception of power', what must be explored is the question of the techno-logy in which this juris-diction consists. And this means that even though we are talking about one and the same techno-logy of *hypomnemata* – that is, of the tertiary retentions engendered by grammatization in its ortho-thetic stage – this techno-logy nevertheless engenders *two* distinct modalities of the *one* psycho-social individuation, modalities that are only distinguishable from each other to the degree that they are nevertheless not separable: on the one hand, the juridico-political and public, but also economic, modality; and, on the other hand, the psycho-individual modality of the culture of the philosophical or religious self.

When Foucault, however, speaks about the technology of power, it applies less to the techno-logies emerging from grammatization and from what he himself calls *hypomnemata* as supports of techniques of the self, than it does to those technologies at the origin of what he will call *disciplinary* society – starting from Marx and from technics in the sense according to which the steam engine and the rifle are technical. And yet, *political technology* as such is defined by Foucault as the domain of *technologies of the individual* and of *technologies of the population*, which means both the discretization and particularization and, on the other hand, the statistical homogenization, of the *I* and the *we*: it is a matter of mnemo-techniques and hypomnesic technologies, which form systems with architectural technologies, as for example in prisons and schools, or with instrumental technologies, as with the army and the rifle, but which constitutes the concrete implementation, each time historically singular, of the process of grammatization, *which, for us, includes the machine*, and which forms systems with the technical system in general.

While I have enlarged the concept of grammatization so that it includes mechanized discretization, including the discretization of gestures in the history of tertiary retention and mnemo-technics[59]

– which leads to the digitalization of mnemo-technological machines strictly speaking, and to what one calls today cognitive technologies, which for me equally qualify as spiritual technologies – it is also necessary to enlarge, inversely, the technologies of biopolitical and disciplinary power analysed by Foucault, in order to include *hypomnemata* in all their forms, including mechanized forms. And this is what, it seems, Foucault lacked the time to do, a fact that is all the more strange, given that he did not cease to practise archivistic technology, which he investigates in *The Order of Things*.[60] As for the technology of the self, Foucault analyses this in 'Self Writing', which begins in the following way:

> These pages are part of a series of studies on 'the arts of oneself,' that is, on the aesthetics of existence and the government of oneself and of others in the Greco-Roman culture during the first two centuries of the empire.[61]

It is therefore clear that in 1983 it was *also* a matter of studying the government of others – before the death of Foucault, a work was planned for publication by Seuil, with the title *Le Gouvernement de soi et des autres*.[62]

Before returning to the techniques of *otium* that constitute specific usages of *hypomnemata* – in relation to which it is nevertheless necessary to note that registers and account-books are also what capitalist innovators will utilize in order to develop rational accounting and a new comprehension of reason as *ratio*, the latter being understood in the accountancy sense – it is necessary to examine more closely what Foucault wrote about technologies of power in general.

Technologies of micro-powers exceeding the sphere of juridical and state power do not aim to be interdictive, but are rather aimed at efficiency and production. These micro-powers undergo a profound mutation at the moment disciplinary societies appear, necessitated by the fact that monarchical power systems were beset by two major inconveniences. On the one hand, the nets which they formed were too wide and let through:

> an almost infinite number of things, elements, conducts and processes.[63]

On the other hand, they were onerous and always proceeded by 'economic subtraction'[64] – which means that they reduced the speed of economic flow.

Foucault here calls for an *enlarged* consideration of technology and argues, in particular, that it not be confined to the steam engine or even to the tool: it is a matter of identifying techniques that constitute a political technology, diverse techno-logies constituting discipline directed first of all towards the control of individuals, and as such forming a 'political anatomy'. Bentham's panopticon belongs to this family of political technologies, which one sees at work in education, in the school as an institution of training and of the incorporation of discipline into the body of the pupil, beneath the gaze of the teacher – as the prisoner is beneath the gaze of the warden. And there are also, then, biopolitical technologies, concerning the management of populations,

> technologies that did not target individuals as individuals. [. . .] We discover that that on which power is exercised is the population [. . .], living beings, traversed, commanded, ruled by processes and biological laws.[65]

One can only underline here the continuity with what marketing implements via the culture industries, and again insist on the convergence between hypomneses and technologies insofar as, with digitalization, this convergence enables the passage from disciplinary societies to control societies, which Deleuze will analyse towards the end of his life. But it is also necessary to recognize that the capturing, harnessing and exploitation of libidinal energy, for which the culture industries are functional organs, also involves a rupture: this harnessing of flux is no longer coercive but voluntary – in the sense that what develops is a voluntary servitude. The distinction that Deleuze proposes between disciplinary and control societies lies, before anything else, in this rupture. But what must then be shown is why control society, as the industrial exploitation of libidinal energies, is inevitably a society of techniques of desubjectivation, of disindividuation, and a society that rapidly exhausts its own viability, reliability [*fiabilité*], *engagement* [*fiance*], trust [*confiance*] and belief – that which we already find ourselves in the midst of living.

12. The constitution of the self and European constitution

Now, understanding this means grasping that control technologies pursue and refine the goals of biopolitical technologies, in order to make of the population:

> a machine for producing, producing riches, goods, producing other individuals.

And this occurs at the cost of a transformation and eventually a decomposition of the process of psycho-social individuation. Foucault describes here the becoming-mass that begins even before the industrial revolution, and of which the embryonic stage consists in the appearance of disciplinary individuation, both the anatomization of the trainable, individual body, and the homogenization and identification of the body of populations as manageable ensembles of living human potentials [*puissances*]:

> There were two great revolutions in the technology of power: the discovery of discipline and the discovery of the regulation and perfection of an anatomo-politics and the perfection of a bio-politics.[66]

But when it comes to control societies, it is not merely a matter of making the population into a production machine: it is a matter of making it into a consumer market, and the training involved becomes that of consumer behaviour – and it is for this reason that it is a matter of desubjectivation, that is, a programmed destruction of the singularity of *savoir-vivre*. Now, in this process, the 'bourgeoisie' is itself progressively absorbed: it is itself desubjectivated by the very biopolitical technologies it implements. It is, in the same stroke, affected in its turn by demotivation, loss of trust and disbelief. It is in this way that the very idea of the bourgeoisie, whether 'petty' or 'grand', becomes obsolete, after the annihilation of the nobility. This process concretizes what I call generalized proletarianization, from which there is no longer any escape: the grammatized retentional milieu that constitutes the world in general, and that configures mental and affective equilibria as much as economic and social equilibria, is entirely polluted and affects the entire population, just as a Parisian suffers the toxicity of the atmosphere regardless of his or her social condition.

The biopolitical technologies described by Foucault essentially control the body, and constitute as such a political anatomy and a biopolitics of populations. But this is not yet a matter of a control society, insofar as a control society does not only consist in the installation, throughout society, of social control, but rather penetrates into consciousness, through which it harnesses libidinal energy and thus reinstantiates corporal control, not only by harnessing conscious time but by soliciting the unconscious through the channelling of conscious time, all of which is con-cretely expressed as a new stage of the grammatization of corporal behaviour: the stage characterized by the consumer of the hyper-industrial epoch. And in this regard, between the 'social control' of magical society, of which myths were the regulatory organs, but where the body had not yet been denied by opposing it to the soul, and the social control of 'disenchanted' society, in which statistics liquidated belief as the condition of regulation, and where the body returns as body, as flesh, as labour-force, there is a rupture that passes precisely through the grammatization of bodies, of which machines, producing the proletariat, are the central moment, and around which technologies of power arrange themselves, as described by Foucault.

Foucault's analysis of biopolitical technologies, however, which appeared in 1976, failed to establish any relation to the second technological revolution of grammatization, which conditions the rationalization described by Weber, and this failure is all the more striking given that Foucault speaks precisely of grammatization in his analysis of *hypomnemata* in 'Self Writing', dating from 1983. Now, what he describes in his analysis of the *ascetic* and, more precisely, *monastic* practices of *hypomnemata* is the way in which these hypomnesic techno-logies constitute the process of psychic individuation, which is taken to its limit as *ethopoiesis*:

> [W]riting constitutes an essential stage in the process to which the whole *askesis* leads: namely, the fashioning of accepted discourses, recognized as true, into rational principles of action. As an element of self-training, writing has, to use an expression that one finds in

Plutarch, an *ethopoietic* function: it is an agent of the transformation of truth into *ethos*.[67]

But this transformation *of the truth* is a transformation *of the self*. It is an *individuation* (a 'subjectivation'): hypomnesic practices, which are features of what the Romans called *otium*, and which Luther will condemn and Calvin even more so, and after him Franklin, *constitute the soul* properly speaking, the *psyche*, and must as such

> form part of ourselves: in short, the soul must make them not merely its own but itself.

The final goal of their assembly

> is nothing less than the constitution of the self.[68]

It is here a question of constitution. And here, where one must pass from psychic individuation to psychic *and* collective individuation, the question of a politics of *hypomnemata* necessarily arises, insofar as this is what makes possible the constitution of the self, supported by a constitution of the *we* insofar as this is a properly political constitution, insofar as this is the foundation of a new stage of psychic and collective individuation corresponding to its particular mnemo-technological epoch. This is the level on which the question of a European constitution must today be posed.

Now, such a constitution must revisit, analyse and overcome the consequences of what – from Luther to Franklin, and passing through Calvin – the practice of *hypomnemata* has turned into, insofar as the practice of the *self*, and the constitution of the *we*, have been essentially reduced to a system of *ratio*, that is, of accounting instruments, and to a system of harnessing the libido aimed precisely at the liquidation of the psychic *self*, which can only lead to the liquidation not merely of the political *self* but also, and inevitably, of the economic *self*, that is, to the liquidation of all trust and all belief.

Monasticism, as epoch of psychic and collective individuation – collective since religious – was a perpetuated and major (particularly during the Middle Ages) institutionalization of *mélétè*,[69] that is, of discipline as defined by the Stoics, and of those practices of *otium* which then become religious – for both regular and secular orders, that is, concerning both the clergy and the faithful in general. Christianity perhaps constituted as such a separation between the nobility of the conquering warrior and the nobility of the clergy that combats itself – that is, that is turned towards the possibility of its elevation. This elevation can, certainly, turn against itself in renouncing life, and what Nietzsche denounces is precisely this aspect of that institutionalization that consists in spreading Christianity as a form of *popular Platonism*, that is, as metaphysics, leading inevitably to nihilism, and to the massification of weakness, while Marx, as is well known, sees in the *otium* of the people its opium.

Moreover, *otium* – as the culture of that of which we must take care – remains the permanent question of philosophers, in frequently opposed forms. Montaigne clearly represents a philosophical resurgence of the question of *mélétè* and of its *hypomnemata* at the end of the Renaissance. But *no* philosopher escapes the question of asceticism, of measure, and of a difference that requires discussion, culture, 'consciousness' or affirmation – the question of an *unconditioned*, of an *exception*, and of an *other plane*, for example of a *plane of consistence*, in short, of an 'extra-ordinariness' of things that nihilism, however, evens out. And it is not an accident that the first two great philosophical movements following the Presocratics, and in that war about grammatization between philosophy and sophistry during the life and after the condemnation to death of Socrates, were, before anything else, *schools*: places of elevation, places where pupils were raised.

Nobility and clergy, conquerors and clerics, cultivate elevation towards the best, the potential of the best, its power, but also its act – and this difference between potential and act is, precisely, something to which I shall return: this culture is that of an aristocracy, everybody else constituting yokels [*les manants*], whether they are bourgeois (urban), that is, commoners and plebeians, or whether they are peasants, that is, serfs. The advent of Luther constitutes a complete change in this regard. And beyond this, capitalism, effacing the distinction that it is helpful to make between subsistence and existence, and, even further, generalizing proletarianization, finally absorbs the world of clerics into its functions and its forces of production just as it controls all sensible life, by replacing sensible experience of singularity with the aesthetic conditioning of consumer behaviour. Now, all this is tied to grammatization, from the Bible that the Protestant henceforth reads alone within his home, up until the hyper-cultural industries of the digital age, passing by way of books and account-books that enable the development of a 'rational' *negotium*.

13.   'In God we trust': belief and trust in the 'work ethic'

The spirit of capitalism changes the meaning of elevation, of the desire to raise oneself up: it becomes a 'work ethic', that is, an ethic of *negotium*. But this is equally a transformation of the very idea of culture: this ethic is a new comprehension of culture – leading to cultural capitalism, which amounts to the pure and simple liquidation of culture understood as that which dedicates a cult or as that which cultivates and *practises* a *difference*, a difference that we must *make*, of which the distinction between *otium* and *negotium* was the great historical figure in Roman Christianity, but which can already be found in Socratic discourse, when Socrates speaks of his *mélété thanatou* – of his existence as learning to die.

With the advent of capitalism, issuing from a new stage of grammatization, which is also a new epoch of Western psychosocial individuation, we must however *adapt* to a system that no longer has any need for support from any religious force, and this adaptation substitutes for all other motivation the necessity of what is called the cult of accumulation, that is, of capitalization as generalized calculability. Now, such a cult is self-destructive: it is irrational in the sense that it destroys *motives*, for which it substitutes *addictions*. And this means that the calculation of trust leads to disbelief and miscreance, and ruins trust itself. The rational development of trust – rational understood here as accountable – leads to the destruction of rational belief, the destruction, by *ratio* as particularization of all singularities, of *logos* understood as motive, that is, also, and I will return to this in the final chapter, of *theos*, of that which according to Aristotle animates each soul, as absolute singularity.

The rational development of trust is therefore irrational. This is the meaning and the final consequence of the absorption of the practices of *hypomnemata* – previously devoted to *otium* as cult of the absoluteness of the singularity of existence, that is, as cult of what I characterize as that which constitutes the *consistence* of existence – into *negotium*, as efficiency of calculation rationalizing all layers of existence, such that existence thereby becomes nothing more than the struggle for survival, reduced to the busyness of subsistence.

This being so, elevation, as *eris*, that form of competition [*émulation*] which in Greek tragedy is turned towards the *ariston*, is what, degraded by the ideology of trust [*confiance*], becomes the theory of competition [*concurrence*], conceived no longer as elevation but as levelling, lowering, as the constitution of *trust* [in English]. And hence the game of calculated capitalist trust involves a new paradox, given that the game of competition is in principle guaranteed by anti-trust laws. Now, the reality is that the production of *trust* [in English] as calculated trust necessarily results in the *trust* [in English] as monopoly, that is, as entropy: calculation is that which eliminates all negentropy, all singularity, all opacity, as Jean-François Lyotard saw very well. And *trust* [in English], being substituted for *belief* [in English], leads inevitably to degradation, to decadence, to the encouragement of equally degraded and degrading behaviours – in the sense that, whereas *eris* designates competition [*concurrence*] as co-occurrence of occurrences, as the *arena* [*concours*] *in which singularities compete in concert*, that is, in the dialogue [*concertation*] that is *this concerted action in which psycho-social individuation consists* (in Simondon's sense), confidence [*confiance*] as calculation constitutes *trusts* which corrode all confidence and all belief and are at the same time self-destructive.

We have seen that workers whose pay is increased tend to reduce rather than increase the time they spend labouring, in order that they might exist within their own free time, rather than merely survive and subsist. And we have further seen that this contradicts the 'spirit of capitalism', and thus that it was necessary to lower salaries in order to make workers work – and it was for this reason that proletarianization was analysed and understood essentially as pauperization, which does indeed accompany it in the nineteenth century. But with Fordism, as a new industrial as well as political model, the producer becomes, at the beginning of the twentieth century in the United States, a consumer. Everyone, or nearly everyone, gaining a salary, this *everyone* essentially comes to constitute 'the market'. A *new rationality* thus appeared, the expansion of which will be all the more necessary within what affirms itself as *industrial* democracy, even though the Great Depression of the 1930s will appear to be the sudden expression of the 'contradictions of capitalism'. It is at this moment that marketing becomes king, and that the process of proletarianization of the consumer begins, while at the same time *credit begins to be made available to consumers* and not merely to investors.

But this credit is going to irresistibly become 'lifetime value' [in English]:[70] an investment in the consumer as constituting a *lifetime*, insofar as they can be sustainably inscribed within the vast circuit of desubjectivated subsistence, because they are entirely enslaved to the subjectivation of an industrial group. The lifetime of a consumer thus becomes, in turn, a calculable value. This induces, however, the standardization of *savoir-vivre*, that is, the loss of knowledge of how to live, in particular through the service economy that delegates the consumer's existence to bibles (bibles being understood here in the managerial sense according to which they explain precisely how to serve a customer, as, for example, in fast-food restaurants). This, then, constitutes the stage of generalized proletarianization, the impoverishment of existence as well as subsistence, an impoverishment imposed on every individuality, whether psychic or collective, and where all of these individualities are faced with a permanent pressure aiming to particularize and de-singularize them. Now, this situation culminates by engendering a *collapse of reason*, if one understands by 'reason' that which constitutes the motive to live of those souls that Aristotle called 'noetic', and that he also qualified as 'political' to the degree that they are turned towards and inclined towards *philia*. It is this motive that Aristotle named *theos*: Aristotle is par excellence the advent of the onto-theologico-political.

Given that the proletarianizing rationalization of the producer is that which – passing by way of the transformation of *logos* into *ratio*, and as the concrete expression of the 'death of God' – substitutes for the question of belief that of trust, then it turns out that it is the dollar bill that expresses the entirety of the thinking of Benjamin Franklin, that dollar bill on which is inscribed '*In God we trust*', belief having become, according to the sermons of Franklin, legitimately calculable. Such is the result of this new state of mind in which consists the development of capitalism as the permanent invention – literally fascinating – of new modes of production and consumption that must develop counter to tradition, and that presuppose the development of an essentially calculable trust. This calculable trust collides with belief until, finally, it collapses in shock: the artificial fabrication of trust has today become an obsession for the 'managers' and administrators of the production and consumption apparatus, even though it is perfectly clear that this fabrication of trust will encounter the kind of limit that characterizes every addictive situation, and this encounter is, indeed, sooner or later, inevitable. The more one confirms the necessity of maintaining trust, the more one multiplies the artifices, the less trust is in fact established – and one feels all the more the welling up of a frightening mistrust, while at the same there arise frightening planetary *trusts* [in English].

Today (but this begins in the first half of the twentieth century), the *libido*, *desire* in the Freudian sense, and not simply *interest* in the Weberian sense, has become the object of calculation with a view towards systematic exploitation, and this is what makes possible a third revolution of grammatization, after that which opened the age of the Reformation and of the 'innovators' studied by Weber. And at the beginning of the twenty-first century the liquidation of singularities and the resulting tendential destruction of the libidinal economy, of which everybody has a presentiment, even if they deny it, induces both a complete loss of trust by those who have been proletarianized, and the calculating and established disbelief and miscreance of the powerful, who become ever more hegemonic and arrogant. Total proletarianization has as its counterpart generalized discredit, and this threatens the capitalist system at its very heart: the rational development of trust leads to the rational destruction of all belief insofar as this is essential to any future, which can only ever be indeterminate, singular, exceptional and incalculable – and negentropic at this unique price, which is beyond measure, an inestimable price, a difference without possible comparison, without a yardstick, that primordial excess through which Bataille attempts to think 'general economy', the necessity of which Nietzsche affirms as the exception counter-ing the herdish massification inducing the adaptation in which the reign of nihilism consists. This inestimable price is the condition of *excess*, that is, the condition of all economy not enslaved to immediate subsistence – or, in other words, of all civilization. If Valéry can be found to say that all civilizations are mortal, then we are in the course of living a new mortality of civilization. But I have begun this book by posing that this mortality is a *catastro-phe*, which means that it must open up a new stage of psycho-social individuation that it is the task of contemporary political economy to invent, in accordance with that becoming of *hypomne-mata* in which consists contemporary industrial development.

If nihilism, in fact, is this destruction of all belief, that is, also, of all exception, an event intrinsically tied to the development of the spirit of capitalism as an accountable consequence of the second revolution of grammatization, and then tied to the deploy-ment of industrial mechanization, which is another age of gram-matization, and which remains entirely to be thought, then, faced with this event, Nietzsche calls for another belief, as has been underlined by Marc Crépon:

> To what does one say 'yes' when one deliberately renounces all forms of appropriation? Nietzsche's response is without ambiguity: one says 'yes' to a new 'belief'.[71]

14. Subsistence, existence and consistence

Nothing in our time is more necessary than a new interrogation of the theologico-political, since the new question of belief in politics is not a return to the religious but the return of that which was suppressed through the death of God, and which, perhaps, will only become stronger, with the force of a phantom, if it is true that when the father is killed he becomes stronger and returns as a phantom. This is the question of *consistence*, insofar as that which does not exist *cannot* become an object of calculation – the question of consistence insofar as it means that which distinguishes, but does not oppose, motive and *ratio*. This is the question of that which, as existence turned towards the consistent *which does not exist*, and which, as such, is always already projected beyond mere subsistence, composes (with) the incalculable:

> One must have had in the poem a number such that it prevents counting.[72]

In other words, *it is not only God who, though not existing, consists.* It is also art, justice, ideas in general. Justice certainly does not exist on Earth, and will never exist. Who, however, would dare to suggest that this idea does not consist, and does not merit being *maintained*, and even *cultivated* in young souls, whom one *raises* on this basis, precisely *because* justice does not exist? Who would dare to maintain that because, *in fact*, justice does not exist, we should therefore *renounce* the desire for justice? Ideas *in general*, and not only the idea of justice, whatever these ideas may be, do not exist: they are only made to consist.

There are certainly diverse modalities of the inexistence of ideas: the idea of the triangle does not 'inexist', that is, does not consist, in the same way as the idea of the bee, which does not consist in the same way as God, who does not consist in the same way as the *beautiful*, or as *the* virtuous, which does not consist in the same way as *the* French language. If *the* French language does not exist any more than *the* bee, *ways* of speaking French do exist, just as *bees* exist in the plural; however, what distinguishes two ways of speaking French from two ways of being a bee is very different and even incomparable: the way of speaking French is *constituted* by its *idiomatic difference* in relation to other ways, which is not the case for the bee in relation to other bees, but rather in relation to other insects. As for God, he does not exist at all, which does not prevent him from consisting, at least in certain souls. And as for beauty, it is constituted in still another modality, which is what Kant calls reflective judgement – and I say, in my own language, that it only exists by default: its existence consists in the very fact that it causes *faults* or is *deficient* [*fait défauts*]. Of virtue, we must say that it is first defined as the elevation or the nobility of a singularity that is, precisely, incomparable and, as such, never ex-sists. The triangle, finally, can be said to constitute a mathematical ideality, which constitutes a world, that of mathemes, but this world, which does not exist, is nevertheless within a mode of inexistence completely other than the idea of God: it *founds* science.

Such is the force of ideas or, as Freud said, their power. Such is the power of knowing, of sapidity, sapience – all of which has been profoundly redistributed since the death of God, and since, as a consequence, philosophers no longer seek to demonstrate the proof of his existence. God being dead, the devil is nevertheless still very much alive, and, as *Beruf* of the *trust* [in English] ingesting and eliminating all *belief* [in English], he risks ruining forever the ineluctable becoming-industrial of the world.

To put this in another way, ideas are defective [*font défaut*]. It is nevertheless and first of all a matter of not demonizing this devil, which is also that force in the play of forces that gives ideas their force: we need to calculate trust as much as we need to presuppose belief, belief in the dia-chrony in which singularity consists, and that is also always turned towards the *diabelein* that supports all faith in its bosom, beginning with that *faith in oneself* that supports the singular being. But it is a matter of combating the *hegemony* of calculating trust, which is *autophagous*, and can only engender discredit. Because if the death of God, that is, the revelation of his inexistence, is not inevitably the nullification of the question of consistence, then we must nevertheless say that with the development of the spirit of capitalism, the becoming calculable of that which *projected*, as existences (as singularities), consistences (the ideas, knowledges and their powers), this becoming [*devenir*], without the future [*avenir*] with which it is not automatically synonymous, is that which tends to reduce these consistences to ashes: ashes of inexistent and inconsistent subsistences. To the insipid.

In fact, the difference – which I have not ceased to maintain here, while nevertheless striving to avoid turning it into an opposition – between subsistence and existence, presupposes in its turn a difference between existence and consistence. This is, moreover, what Heidegger's *ontological difference* attempts to think, after the death of God. But Heidegger, like Plato, rejects *hypomnesis,* and fails to understand what difference the question of care makes to the *practice* of *hypomnemata* – he sees nothing of the process of grammatization; nor even that what he calls *Dasein* is also a process of *psychic and collective* individuation, all of which will lead him astray when it comes to the question of a *people*. He is led back to a *metaphysical* conception of this difference, making it into an *opposition* – the opposition between *Besorgen*, which one translates into French as 'preoccupation', that is, *negotium*, and *Sorge*, that is, *otium*: the opposition between calculated time and *Eigentlichkeit*. In brief, with the ontological difference Heidegger fails to think tertiary retention, through which consistence *constitutes itself*, as protention, that is, as the temporalization in which consists the individuation of that which remains always to come.

Consistence is, in fact, an archi-protention: what I will call a *collective secondary protention*, that projects itself in and from *collective secondary retentions*, which will be analysed in the following chapter.[73] *Cultivating* the difference between consistence and existence – this difference being the singular, that is, *incomparable*, and in this sense inexistent, reality (if by existing one understands calculable) of that difference, itself *improbable* (that is, which we do not know how to prove), between existence and subsistence – *cultivating this difference* is what the hyperindustrial control of tertiary retention and, through this process, the control of individual and collective secondary retention (I shall return to this), has made impossible.

Because retentional *practices* alone permit protentional projections, that is, the satisfaction of desires, like the desire to elevate oneself in which desire always consists – including desires such as those for the 'experience of limits', the savagery and delights of the fall: the fall only procures such a delight as a kind of knowledge that is then preliminary to elevation. Marketing, on the other hand, substitutes mere *usages* [in English] for these practices, usages that aim to use products and with them consumers, to consume the time through which they consume themselves – this is what must be combated. Like the *hegemony* of the *restricted economy*, this consumption must be combated, and requires a *general economy*,[74] that is, a political economy that renews the question of the belief in politics.

Now, this presupposes before anything else the critique of 'post-modern' mythology that, as *ideology*, has made the consideration of the question of the relation between *otium* and *negotium* impossible. I would therefore now like to turn to the myth of the 'leisure society', also called 'post-industrial society', a myth that presumes to declare the disappearance of the proletariat and the advent of the middle classes, whereas the truth is, on the contrary, that the control of libidinal energy is devoted to generalized proletarianization and the herdish accomplishment of nihilism in hyper-industrial society.

3

The *Otium* of the People

[A]t an ideological level [. . .] capitalism will face increasing difficulties, if it does not restore some grounds for hope to those whose engagement is required for the functioning of the system as a whole.

We call the ideology that justifies engagement in capitalism 'spirit of capitalism'.

People need powerful moral reasons for rallying to capitalism.

Competitive private enterprise is always deemed more effective and efficient than non-profit-making organizations (but this is at the undisclosed price of transforming the art lover, the citizen, the student, children with respect to their teachers, from recipients of social services into . . . consumers).

Luc Boltanski and Ève Chiapello[1]

Ancient, yet still alive, this multicenturied past flows into the present like the Amazon River pouring into the Atlantic Ocean the vast flood of its cloudy waters.

Fernand Braudel[2]

1.   Postmodern renunciation and the quantum leap

Decadence is a de-composition of the forces of individuation and of all the individualities that must compose it, including collective economic individualities (a corporation, which is a collective economic individual, is thus a case of social individuation). In this *proliferous* decomposition, *ressentiment* prevents thinking of the composition of forces, and prevents the affirmation of their *lack of unity* [*défaut d'unité*] (and the lack of identity, of calculability, and of the determination of the individuation that results from it) as a *chance*: as a chance within that game that consists in the *pursuit* of individuation in metastability. The decomposition of tendencies is the decomposition of metastability as that which joins the synchronic and the diachronic. This decomposition causes the loss of individuation as much as it is its result, so that what is involved here is a vicious circle: the loss of individuation results from the hyper-synchronization that follows from the becoming-hegemonic of the tendency towards synchronization, that is, from the *elimination* of that diachrony that is singularity, and, as the destruction of primordial narcissism, this feeds resentment, which in its turn intensifies decomposition. The explosion of conflict is everywhere threatening: social conflicts, geopolitical conflicts, religious conflicts, inter-ethnic conflicts, and so on.

It remains the case that if a *thought* and *practice* of the composition of forces are more urgent than ever, then it is nevertheless also the case that to think and act by composition does not mean renouncing *opposing* oneself to decomposition. Now, there is, today, another temptation: at the end of the twentieth century, reigning 'postmodernism', acting from out of a collapse in the belief in progress – that is, also, a collapse in the belief in politics – eventually turned this state of affairs into an historic truth, and thus got itself mired in a renunciation, with the consequence that to want to think about the course things were taking came to appear derisory. The whole world today knows very well, however, that abandoning things to their course is, within our current situation, *suicidal*: the fact that this epoch is *decadent* means that it has run its course [*révolue*], and to not act is to renounce life. This decadence, however, *also* means that the epoch is exhausted – that it stagnates, that it is unable to engender its own transformation. In other words, this means that it requires a *jumpstart* [*sursaut*] – let's say, to remain with the language of Simondon, a *quantum* leap [*un sursaut quantique*]. This leap could only be an *opposition* to decomposition.

Who, however, still believes in the possibility of such a leap, who would deny that it is already too late, and that it is futile to attempt to interrupt the course of things and *act out their revolution*, that is, to publicly establish the fact that, given that this course has run its course, it must be a matter of *inaugurating* not only a new stage of the process of individuation but in fact another epoch of individuation, a story that follows on from this *catastrophe* by installing a new order of things, or, in brief, the fact that it is a matter of *making* this revolution? If it is quite clear that no one is able to believe in this possibility, it is also quite clear that only a *new belief* in this possibility *could* make it possible, while the temptation to claim that things must follow their course up until their *final* catastrophe, that is, until there is no tomorrow, induces an unbearable *lethargy* of thought. It is impossible to accept such resignation, which is itself a consequence of this decomposition. The necessary leap opposing it is the question of will and of belief.

Contrary to a widespread delusion, belief only exists where there is a *will* to believe. Belief is that which is *maintained* and *produced*: it is not a given of individual spontaneity. And the will to believe, which belief presupposes, does not secrete a psychic *subject* but a *process* of psycho-social individuation, characterized by practices and behavioural controls, a social control that can also become, as an epoch of the process of adoption that is always a process of individuation, and through the intermediary of technologies of grammatization, a control society, no longer containing anything other than usages. But at this point, and this is my central thesis, there is no longer any belief in nor possibility of a pursuit of individuation.

Will has always been conceived as the faculty of a subject, that is, as an avatar of the metaphysics of representation that has reigned since the birth of modern philosophy. It has, in other words, been conceived as an avatar of onto-theologico-political thought, which is, precisely, a thought incapable of thinking becoming, since it does not see in becoming anything other than an accident of being, that is, an illusion. This is the reason that will has become, in the course of the last few decades, an outmoded theme, seeming to constitute nothing more than a lure. The Nietzschean question of nihilism, however, is more profoundly that of will, and of thinking will *after* the liquidation of the onto-theologico-political – of a will to power of which the operational concept is here, for us, individuation as process. Because, accord-

ing to my proposed reading of the Nietzschean question of nihilism, this question of will, which is not at all outmoded, is that
which the de-composition of tendencies, that is, the ruin of individuation, tends to liquidate, at the precise point where it is a
matter of *engaging in combat*, of opposing this hegemony, and
of affirming the will to will – this is what I have named the
quantum leap.

In spite of this, this discourse of the will to will, inspired by
Nietzsche and revisited by Simondon, does not merely seem like
an outmoded lure: it appears eminently dangerous. It sounds at
the same time like the discourse on the will and the discourse on
power that was addressed to the German people in 1933. It is for
this reason that we tend to conclude that when philosophy, as
extreme critique of metaphysics, transforms itself into political
thought, whether we are speaking of *class struggle*, of the *will to
power*, or of *resolution*, we can only expect the worst. We are
aware these days that to search for the best leads to the worst,
and we therefore fear to act. We know, and have learned, through
books, films, newspapers, and through our own existence, the
Terror of 1793, Stalinism and Nazism. We have seen the greatest
thinkers, and in particular Marx, Nietzsche and Heidegger, either
inspire totalitarian organizations, or allow themselves to be
deluded by such mirages, leading to abominable catastrophes.
Each time, these regimes echo concepts of struggle, of will or of
Entschlossenheit.

We have even come to think that 'metaphysics' – in what one
calls metaphysics in the Kantian sense, then in the Heideggerian
sense, and that affects philosophy in its totality, Kant and Heidegger
included – amounts to the loss by philosophy of its object and
even of its way of seeking it, as the Platonic discourse *opposing*
the sensible and the intelligible, that is, the body and soul, that
is, mortal and immortal, then as the Cartesian discourse of
the will to mastery and possession of nature, then as Hegelian
discourse on the end of history and fulfilment of spirit in the dia-
lectic of will and mastery, but also as philosophy wishing to
establish phenomenology as rigorous science, or as the propriety
of the proper or authenticity, that is, as *Eigentlichkeit*. We have
come to think that everything that is diversely yet constantly
metaphysical *as the play of oppositions* is an historical element

essential to the advent of nihilism, and of what I describe here as de-composition.

We have therefore lost our trust in thought for action – because we think, with reason, that an action always passes through a moment of opposition. We would like to *be able to think without having to act*, and *to be able to act without having to think*. We would like to think that *discourse* could *justify the world* while having nothing to *fear* in this world, and that the *world* can continue to *follow its course* while having nothing to *expect* of thought or of its discourse that could interrupt or divert this course.

Unfortunately, the world does not follow its course: it becomes squalid, un-world [*im-monde*]. And discourse can no longer *justify* this accumulation of physical and symbolic hideousness [*immondices*] and of human waste that our planet is in the process of becoming. Because, today, we *also* know that the worst more and more frequently accompanies liberalism, the reach of which has become irreversibly planetary, and that the worst of liberalism has direct effects, even in the heart of industrial democracies, as well as indirect effects, but which are in fact far more unjust, in those countries that it pillages, against which it makes war, or that it kills with all kinds of poison and pollution. This *new reign of the worst* is, in its final consequences, the reign of disbelief or miscreance in all its forms, including and especially all forms of fundamentalism (which is its inverse), whether religious fundamentalism (which denounces, precisely, the 'unbelievers' [*mécréants*], and finds its credit in doing so), or secular fundamentalism (which denounces this denunciation, but in doing so renounces the question of *where* credit could any longer be found).

2.   Passage to the act, will and power

Today, *there is nothing worse than to fail to think about action.* That is, also, and in all its forms, best and worst, transgression, the *passage to the act*; and power [*puissance*], including, and first of all, that which the phrase 'will to power' tries to think; and the *difference* between act and potential [*puissance*].

Power, in the analyses I have proposed of the time of existence and of individuation, is what I have called epiphylogenesis, that is, *tekhné* as that which supports and transmits pre-individual milieus inherited by the *I* and the *we*, which produce, in other words, individuations, and of which the *act* is precisely individuation insofar as it is always *at once* psychic and collective: insofar as it is always the composition of the synchronic and the diachronic as tendencies.

Action is always in some way such a passage to the act of a potential – such a *passage*: from potential to act – which means that action is always in some way *technical*, that is, also, *practical*. To think about action is equally, as has long been thought, to think the relation of theory and practice. But what I must state here, with Heidegger, as well as with Marx, is that this must mean thinking theory *as* practice, and practice as *theorein*: as contemplation. In brief, it is a matter of thinking practice as that which the Romans called *otium*.

But it must then be asked: how does technics fit into this picture? The answer is very clear: technics is that which, through theory, proceeds from a redoubling of the grammatization of pre-individual funds, which thus become political, hence a redoubling of that grammatization that itself constitutes an epochal technological redoubling.[3] In brief, *theorein* is a *practice* of which the *question* and the necessity appear with the *hypomnesis* that writing constitutes. And this is why, as we have seen with Foucault, the culture of the self, that is, precisely, *otium*, is first of all a practice of *hypomnemata*, that is, a technique of the self.

Otium is that which is not *negotium*: it is that which distinguishes itself – it is a distinction. That is, it is the discernment of a difference – of a difference that only exists to the extent that one *believes* in it, and that one only believes to the extent that one *makes* it, all of this signifying, more exactly, that the difference *is not and does not become that which is and such as one makes it* except to the extent that one *cultivates* it, *that is, to the extent that one wants it*: one does not contemplate, as *theorein*, unless one practises it, unless one *makes it be*, that is, *become*, and *grow*, and *raise itself*, rather than 'letting it be'.

As for *negotium*, this is not simply the commerce of commodities (*otium* being able itself to be a commerce – in particular a symbolic commerce). Rather, it is human commerce in general, but insofar as it is submitted in general to the imperative of subsistence, and insofar as it can render *inaccessible* the dignity of existence. This is commerce as business, thus it is that to which Heidegger was referring with the term *Besorgen*, that which, insofar as it is preoccupation, is in some way remotely controlled by usages defined in relation to a norm based entirely on the notion of utility.

The *practice* of *otium* is what, since the sixteenth century, is called in French, *culture*, as the 'development of the intellectual faculties through appropriate exercises'. One also speaks of physical culture and, in the Greek city, of everything that was practised in the gymnasium as a *place of training*, that gymnasium the name of which is preserved in Germanic civilization – and, when one thinks of this, images spring to mind of the worst, as well as of the best. Culture is, however, in Greece as in France as in the Germanic world, the practice of daily repetitive exercises, practices that constitute a discipline, or what I have called, in restoring an ancient word, a *mélétè*.

The first meaning of all culture is this theoretical *practice*, and, like *otium*, it aims for the best, and is also, therefore, a form of *eris*, a culture of *ariston* – a concern with elevation. This is why the education of children, children as pupils [*élèves*] or insofar as their parents raise them, is an *everyday* [*ordinaire*] and generalized form of this culture, and this is already a form of *otium* insofar as inheriting the authority won by the ascendants is a matter of yielding a profit, rather than merely a matter of aping one's elders (because to merely conserve a heritage is already decadent). And thus we can say that education is an ordinary form of culture, of *otium*, even though strictly speaking *otium* is a practice of that which is *out* of the ordinary, of that which is extra-ordinary.

We have seen that elevation can always turn into its contrary and, as such, as *aim*, it is cast through *elpis*, expectation, or that which I also call protention, which is equally fear: fear of the worst. In this expectation are contained all the benefits, but also all the costs: *elpis*, which is held in Pandora's box, is at the same time, and for *this* reason, hope and fear. But it is precisely *for this reason* that we have to *cultivate* it, by taking care of it through practices that foster trust and hope, for this is the best guarantee we can have of avoiding the installation of fear – *phobos* – fear that inevitably engenders reactivity, resentment, jealousy and *stasis*, as Hesiod says in both *Works and Days* and the *Theogony*.

3. Political laziness, laziness of the spirit and 'leisure society'

It is because he is well aware of this, and equally aware of the fact that culture, or what he calls *esprit*, only survives on the condition of being practical, that *in 1939, that tragic year*, Valéry deplores that:

> all these values, rising and falling, constitute the great stock market of human affairs. Among them, the unfortunate value of *spirit* has not ceased to fall.[4]

Valéry, who sixteen years earlier meditated on the disaster of the First World War, when he saw the evidence of the mortality of civilizations, here feels that a new and immense European disaster is looming, an even worse disaster – because there is always worse than the worst. What does this pronouncement of such a disaster, a disaster described by Valéry as a fall in spirit value [*valeur esprit*], give *us* to think today, *we*, the people living at the turn of the twenty-first century, given that in 1939 television did not yet even exist, and only 45 per cent of the French listened to the radio? And, most importantly, what obligations does this create for us? Whatever the answers to these questions may be, it is not philosophy that causes this disaster: if Nietzsche was able to have been used by the Nazis, if Heidegger was able to believe for a number of months that what he called a 'movement' was an occurrence of his *Entschlossenheit*, nevertheless the disaster in question is first of all, for Valéry, the fact of a *general weakness* of the spirit of which these avatars would merely be cases – and, correlatively, this is a matter of a *political weakness* insofar as it has renounced being a *politics of the spirit* or even a *political economy* of the spirit. Let's be blunt: it is a matter of a *catastrophic laziness of thought* before the fact that:

> a world transformed by the spirit no longer presents to the spirit the same perspectives and directions as before; it poses entirely new problems and countless enigmas.[5]

Such is the case for a new stage of grammatization. And one cannot in fact separate spirit and world, that is, spirit and politics. Philosophy, in particular, is *essentially* a political discourse. And politics, as a modality of the process of individuation, is *essentially* a *care* taken of spirit, of its culture, that is, of a cult of a difference that one must know how to make and maintain, that can be forgotten, and that, when it is forgotten, leads to the worst. This difference is what distinguishes *elevation* from *villainy*. This is the sentiment that accompanies the justice (*dike*) sent by Zeus to mortals, a sentiment that I have called shame [*la vergogne*] in translating *aidos*, and that Deleuze, referring at once to both Primo Levi and Nietzsche, called shame [*la honte*] – 'the shame of being human'.

Just as there is – as I will return to in another work, in turning again to Valéry – a new *spiritual economy*, so there is a politics of the spirit, or rather, there *must* be a politics of the spirit, and this can only be a *political economy* of a spirit proper to the current epoch of grammatization – that being the effective reality of the spirit.

This is the exact way that postmodernism, as an epoch of renunciation, must be analysed, in terms of its discourse about what Jean-François Lyotard, after Alain Touraine, believed could be called '*post-industrial* society'. Postmodern society, he said, is a post-industrial society.[6] If Lyotard knew, in his unique way, that the Freudian question of libidinal economy needed to be reopened, what he nevertheless failed to see was that the heart of this question was the question of consumption, and that consumption constituted a second stage of proletarianization, a stage that Marx himself had been unable to foresee, lacking any idea of this, or of the possibility of thinking the question of a *libidinal* economy. Lyotard, who in *The Postmodern Condition* introduced the idea of a post-industrial age, was unable to continue the thought of capitalist becoming that he had at least commenced in *Libidinal Economy*. Lyotard internalized the ideology of post-industrial society and of the 'leisure society' in which it is supposed to consist, and hence also believed in the disappearance of the proletariat and the coming of the epoch of the middle classes, whereas, on the contrary, the new capitalism, taking hold of computational technologies (a fact about which *The Postmodern Condition* con-

tains analyses that are often magnificent), enlarges the concept of
the proletariat, and concretizes it, while unleashing a new process
of the proletarianization of society: this is what leads to *hyper-industrial* society.

This will not prevent Lyotard from seeing, in what he designates
as a postmodern *condition*, a new age of knowledge, such that,
according to my own analyses, destroying the difference that must
be *made* between *otium* and *negotium* (which must be distinguished, but without *opposing* them), an indifferentiation – which
also constitutes what I have called in *De la misère symbolique 1*
the integration of the world of clerics, that is, also, of the practice
of *hypomnemata*, as mnemo-technics, into the heart of production
– that essentially becomes the implementation of mnemo-*technologies* placed into the service of production as well as of distribution and consumption, together forming an integrated system, and
constituting the infrastructure (which can no longer be distinguished from its superstructure) of a *process of proletarianization
henceforth extended to all modes of existence*, existence being
essentially submitted to the imperatives of subsistence, and *consistence* being *in this way* purely and simply obliterated.

Such is *decadence*. The fact that Lyotard did not criticize the
ideology of leisure meant that, even though he never ceased to
interrogate capitalism about the relation between time and credit,[7]
he was unable to think the question of *belief as a paradox of
capitalism*.

4. The 'leisure society', a lure masking the extension of proletarianization to the consumer

The fable of 'post-industrial society', which has in recent decades
been dominant, has to a great extent seduced political and philosophical thought. According to this fable, that began to be told
after 1968, we have entered into the age of 'free time', that is, into
an individualistic society of leisure. Not only did this fable influence and undermine 'postmodern' philosophy, but it inspired
social democracies to presume that we had passed from the epoch
of mass labour and mass consumption of the industrial age, into
the time of the middle classes, and to presume that the proletariat
is on the way to disappearing.

But the proletariat remains very important, firstly because workers have to a large extent been proletarianized (enslaved to a mechanized system depriving them of initiative and professional knowledge), but also because the proletariat has, in fact, increased in size and, insofar as it names a process, been transformed, such that it now *includes* the middle classes *insofar as they are consumers*, and who are, furthermore, to a large extent pauperized. Contrary to the cliché that a long tradition of political thought of Marxist origin has spread, the proletariat has never been reducible to the working class. The proletarianization of work, as Simondon reformulates it, is a loss of knowledge, that is, a loss of the capacity to individuate oneself. Moreover, as Daniel Bensaïd has put it, it is control of work-time,[8] as the implementation of what Foucault called disciplinary society. At the same time, however, as disindividuation and control of life-time, proletarianization has now extended well beyond merely the world of production; it characterizes the condition of the consumer. It is this that defines, for example, the concept of *lifetime value*.[9]

Speaking (as does the theory of post-industrial society inspiring postmodern thought) of the development of leisure – in the sense of time free of all constraint, of 'absolute availability', as the dictionary says – is to fabricate a counter-truth while internalizing, as it were, the discourse of the culture industries themselves. Because the function of such 'leisures' is not actually to *free* individual time but, on the contrary, to *control* it for the purposes of hyper-massification: these are instruments of a new voluntary servitude. Produced and organized by the culture and programming industries, these instruments called 'leisures' constitute the most ordinary, the most quotidian, the most banal, and the most efficacious organs of control societies. As for control societies, these are passing into their hyper-industrial epoch, developing into a cultural and service-based capitalism that, via computer technology, fabricates every element of our ways of living, transforming daily life in the sense of its immediate interests, standardizing existences through the means of 'marketing concepts' [in English], and doing all of this while pursuing the convergence of the audiovisual, the informational and telecommunications: this is the American multimedia strategy, the genesis of which was summarized in the first chapter.

Purportedly 'post-industrial' society has on the contrary become hyper-industrial and, in so doing, it has integrated into the process of proletarianization not only production (that is, subsistence), but consumption (to which existence tends to be reduced). Just as workers who submit to serving the mechanical tool lose their *savoir-faire* and, through that, their individuality, finding themselves thereby reduced to the condition of the proletariat, so too consumers have today become standardized in their behaviours by the formatting and artificial fabrication of their desires: they lose their *savoir-vivre*, that is, their *possibilities of existence. The possibilities for existing are the possibilities of individuating their singularity*, of projecting it *from the pre-individual funds* that constitute the *we* at the heart of which each one of us exists as an *I*, and in which each one of us can only *believe* to the degree that we *believe in* our own individuation. The individuation of this *we* and the belief in its possibility is conditioned by the latitudes that it offers to the *I*s that constitute it to individuate themselves, that is, to *believe in themselves.*

In 'post-industrial' society, purported to be a society 'of leisure' – *leisure* being a possible translation for *otium* – *savoir-vivre*, which constitutes the everyday aspects of that which forms the object of a culture, is replaced by norms substituting brands [*marques*] of fashion [*modes*], to which Mallarmé gave consideration in *La Dernière Mode*, but these are no longer limited, today, to the acquisition of clothes. The *branded* consumer internalizes a pale imitation of 'the representation of the world', which systematizes a sort of fashioning of the principal moments of their 'existence' – and 'fashion', thus rethought as brand (branding those who wear the brand, like an identificatory marker), now involves everyday products and automobiles and computers, and even services, in addition to clothes and other finery.

Now, this 'representation of the world', this wanting to be branded, participating in the loss of individuation, and as a new stage of proletarianization, is an *interruption* of making-world – of the psychic and collective individuation that a world is. It may be true that an interruption constitutes the potential for a new epoch, being an *epokhé*, and that part of fashion's appeal clearly lies in the fact that it is a seductive force of change, and that this extends to the wish to be branded, and there is indeed a genuine element of enjoyment when the 'middle classes' slip on their gilt sneakers. Today, however, it is the very possibility of pursuing individuation that seems suspended, and such a 'representation of the world' seems to contribute to this decomposition, and to extend the interruption of the modalities of generalized world-making to every social milieu, such that we must speak of a becoming non-world of the world, of a non-making-world, since this world no longer individuates itself – a becoming squalid, unworldly [*im-monde*].

'Rationally' promoted by marketing, the *norms of life* elaborated by brands are not *modes of existence*: they conform to new bibles, such as those we have already mentioned, governing the way business functions at fast-food restaurants, those bibles to which franchise-holders must submit to the letter, under pain of breaking the contract – if not the process. These are *doctrines without doctors, or clerics, or 'ideologues'*, all perfectly innocent, utterly postmodern, and ceaselessly renewed by the need to create obsolescence and stimulate cycles of consumption, doctrines that provide an illusion of dynamism and of transforming the world, a world that is, however, backing into an abyss.

In 1930 Freud wrote that, although endowed by industrial technologies with divine attributes, 'present-day man does not feel happy in his godlike character'.[10] And in 1920, in *Group Psychology and the Analysis of the Ego*, he analysed the way in which crowds are tempted to return to the state of being a horde, inhabited by the death-drive that he had discovered in *Beyond the Pleasure Principle*, and that he would revisit a decade later in *Civilization and Its Discontents*, as totalitarianism, fascism, Nazism and anti-Semitism spread their way across Europe. Rereading these texts, one can only dread the possibility that hyper-industrial society may again lead human beings to the worst extremes – all of these extremisms having been *exported* beyond Europe: depriving them of individuality, it leads herds of beings to lack being [*en mal d'être*] and to lack becoming [*en mal de devenir*], that is, to lack a future [*en défaut d'avenir*]. Such inhuman herds will have a greater and greater tendency to become *furious*.

Now, the culture industries play here a decisive role. And it is very strange that, even though Freud speaks of photography, the gramophone and the telephone, he invokes neither the radio nor (and this is even stranger) the cinema, exploited by both Mussolini and Stalin, and subsequently Hitler, and about which an American senator had in 1912 already declared that 'trade follows films'. Nor is Freud able to imagine television, of which the Nazis performed an experimental public broadcast in April 1935. At the same time, Benjamin analysed what he called 'mass narcissism': the taking control of these media by totalitarian powers. But Benjamin did not seem to grasp any more than Freud the *functional* dimension – in every country, including in the democracies – of the nascent culture industries. In brief, in the 1930s, those who felt the coming of the destructive power of the media (and all power is a destructive force) only saw this as a matter of the risks posed by totalitarian political movements, rather than seeing that a decisive transformation of capitalism was being played out, preparing the way for the liquidation of *savoir-vivre* and of the *otium* that *cultivates* these media and that *they* cultivate.

What all this foreshadows is the absorption of the sphere of clerics into the sphere of production by means of technical transformations, and on this point Lyotard was remarkably lucid: this is what he called the 'performativity of knowledge' in the postmodern epoch, that is, the *total* submission of knowledge to production. It remains the case that, failing to see that the *principal* consequence is *generalized* proletarianization, he failed to identify its political meaning, and was thus unable to draw any practical consequence. The reason to undertake philosophy, however, is in order that practical consequences may indeed be drawn.

5. Capitalism, libidinal economy and the 'psychological poverty of groups'

Edward Bernays, double nephew of Freud, on the other hand, *did* theorize the functional role of what, already in his time, was being constituted as the culture industry. He exploited the immense possibilities for behavioural control of what his uncle called *libidinal economy*, and developed 'public relations', techniques of persuasion inspired by theories of the unconscious, techniques which around 1930 he implemented for cigarette manufacturer Philip Morris – at the very moment when Freud felt that in Europe the death-drive was rising up against civilization. But this seems to bear no relation to what is taking place in America. Except for a very strange remark. At first, Freud claims to be obliged to:

> notice the danger of a state of things which might be termed 'the psychological poverty of groups.' This danger is most threatening where the bonds of a society are chiefly constituted by the identification of its members with one another, while individuals of the leader type do not acquire the importance that should fall to them in the formation of a group.[11]

This psychological poverty or immiseration consists in a levelling [*égalisation*]: at the very moment when, in this work, Freud felt coming the indoctrinated crowds of the 1930s, he also deplored the *levelling* that prevents 'certain personalities with the temperament of leaders' from being able to identify members of society with one another – there are touches here of Nietzsche on the advent of nihilism, and these are, indeed, very bizarre. But Freud then affirms (and the emphasis here is my own) that:

> *the present cultural state of America would give us a good opportunity for studying the damage to civilization which is thus to be feared.* But I shall avoid the temptation of entering upon a critique of American civilization; I do not wish to give an impression of wanting myself to employ American methods.

It is not until the denunciation by Adorno and Horkheimer of the 'American way of life' that the function of the culture industries is truly analysed, apart from the critique of media appearing from the 1910s with Karl Kraus. It is true that the analysis undertaken by Adorno and Horkheimer remains supported by a Kantian conception of schematism (the metaphysical character of which is precisely demonstrated by industrial becoming[12]), and that this prevents the building of a critical project and means the analysis remains to some extent reactive. Nevertheless, Adorno and Horkheimer were the first to understand that the culture industries form a system with industry in general, the function of which consists in fabricating and controlling consumer behaviour through massifying ways of life, and that in this case the question of a *total power* over existence no longer amounts to the question of Stalinism, or fascism, or Nazism, but rather to that of capitalism.

After the Second World War, the theory of 'public relations' became connected to 'research on mobility', with the intention of absorbing excess production – valued at 40 per cent – at the moment of the return of peace, and appealing in turn to the 'subconscious' in order to overcome the difficulties that were encountered by industrialists in their attempts to push Americans to buy what their factories could produce. It was a matter of provoking Americans to adopt new products, just as it was necessary to forge a culture of adoption of immigrants and by immigrants. These *two* processes of adoption had to be reinforced and even integrated,[13] with the objective of consuming constituting the binding between diverse communities, and brands themselves becoming supports for identificatory and community projection in this sense: the concept of the brand as social marker was without doubt elaborated within the context of this dual dynamic.

France, however, had in the nineteenth century already created organs the function of which was to facilitate the adoption of industrial products, with the effect of overturning ways of life, and hence with the additional function of struggling against the resistance inevitably provoked by these upheavals: hence the creation of an information agency by Louis Havas in 1835, and the creation of a 'publicity' agency by Émile de Girardin in 1836. But we must await the appearance of the culture industries (cinema and disk) and especially the programme industries (radio and television) before *industrial temporal objects* can be developed. These industries made it possible to *intimately* control individual behaviour, transforming it into mass behaviour – even though the spectator, *isolated in front of his television*, in a different way than occurs at the cinema, maintains the illusion of solitary leisure.

The hyper-industrial sphere extends to all human activities the compulsive and mimetic behaviour of the consumer, including all those activities that can be subsumed under the heading 'free time'. Everything must become consumable – education, culture and health, as well as washing powder and chewing gum. But the illusion that we must create to install this situation can only prove to be *deceptive*, and to provoke frustration, demotivation, discredit, disgust and destructive impulses. Alone in front of my television, I can always tell myself that I am behaving individually, but the reality is that I am doing just the same as hundreds of thousands of viewers who watch the same programme – a fact of which, deep down, I am well aware. Industrial activity, having become planetary, aims to achieve gigantic economies of scale, and therefore, through appropriated technologies, to control and homogenize behaviour: these technologies are principally the programme industries that ensure this function through industrial temporal objects that are purchased and distributed in order to harness conscious time, the conscious time of viewers who then form audiences, and which can be sold to advertising firms. And this means that idle time, which had been denounced by Benjamin Franklin, has henceforth become useful: it is integrated into the 'spirit of capitalism' – it has again become money, and one can calculate its value in the market of audiences. On the other hand, time is no longer free: it can no longer be devoted to leisure insofar as this constitutes a culture of the singularity of a time of existence, devoted to consistences – that is, to ideas, which do not exist, and which are therefore not calculable – and that amount to the various forms of *otium* practised in the course of the history of Western individuation, and that are the most elevated forms of this individuation process.

The post-industrial fable not only fails to understand that the strength of contemporary capitalism stems from the *simultaneous* control of production and consumption regulating the activities of the masses in totality, but rests on the false idea that the individual and the group are opposites – and that society has become 'individualistic', whereas it has in fact never been so herdish. The individual is that which expresses, and *as exception*, the *power* that the group has to individuate singularities: the fable does not see that the psychic individual can only be at the heart of a psychosocial individuation process, where the individuals only individuate themselves insofar as they *contribute* to social individuation. This *intrinsically* collective individuation is only possible because this individuation is the diachronization of *pre-individual funds*, which are, nevertheless, also the initial synchronic funds *adopted* by singularities that are formed in the process of individuation, insofar as it is the composition of these tendencies that constitutes the metastability of its equilibrium. As the suppliers of the 'leisures' of 'post-industrial' society, the programme industries tend on the contrary to *oppose* synchrony and diachrony, with the goal of producing hyper-synchronizations, the *tendential* result of which is that *singular* appropriations – that is, diachronic appropriations – of the pre-individual funds that programmes constitute, become *impossible*. And the 'leisure' industry also – in order to occlude the suffering produced by non-participation, that is, non-individuation, or else to dazzle while making this at the same time an object of spectacle and of lure – comes at last to invent 'reality television'.

I have shown elsewhere that all this is the case because the programme industries exploit the possibilities proper to industrial temporal objects, through which programme schedules are substituted for what André Leroi-Gourhan called socio-ethnic programmes: these schedules are conceived such that my lived past *tends* to become the same as that of my neighbours, because it is in this way that our behaviour can become herdish in the true sense.

6. Culture as transmission of collective secondary retentions

I have already had several occasions to expound upon the concept of the industrial temporal object. A new aspect of this definition must, however, here be brought to light.

Individuation always consists in a selection, in temporal fluxes which constitute the fabric of my existence, of what I call, after Husserl, *primary retention*, that is, of what I retain and that constitutes my present as what comes to pass, which is also that which passes, and which, as such, becomes my past. That which came to pass is that which came to *me*, and what I retain is therefore that which constitutes the *singularity* of my experience: what I retain is not the same as what my neighbours retain. But if there is a difference between *my* primary retentions and those of my neighbours, even when we live through the same event, this is because we have different experiences: we have previously accumulated differing primary retentions that have meanwhile become our pasts, that is, arrangements of secondary retentions. Now, those retentions that have become secondary then form my selection criteria, so that I then produce,[14] by selecting them, primary retentions that will in their turn become secondary, and that will thereby enrich my experience, that is, my capacity for selecting new retentions, and so on. This process is nothing other than that of individuation.

I only think differently from others, I only feel differently from others, I only desire differently from others, I only see differently from others – in short, I only *exist* – because the retentional process in which I consist is unique, and because this retentional process is *also* a protentional process, that is, it is a process that constitutes horizons of expectation. And that which I retain, from the temporal flow in which an event that happens to me consists, is only a retention to the extent that it is a primary selection that I effect through the use of criteria supplied to me *by* my past, a past constituted by secondary retentions that form at the same time filters and expectations, protentions through which I receive the present. *Elpis* is thus constituted through an experience that I also call *epimetheia*.[15]

But there are, on the other hand, also secondary retentions that I inherit even though they are of experiences I have not myself lived, retentions of that which I have not lived but that I have nevertheless *adopted*: this is the case for everything of which I have been told, of that into which I have been initiated, or of that which I have been taught, of that which forms education and instruction and through which I raise myself above myself, like a dwarf carried on the shoulders of a giant. Such retentions are, *at once, both secondary* – because they have been conceived, selected, projected and lived by others, and have constituted their own pasts, from out of their own presents, such as the *Elements* of Euclid, or, again, *The Remembrance of Things Past* – and *collective, common, inherited* by everyone as the past of everyone. They constitute a pre-individual fund. This is true of works [*oeuvres*], whatever they may be, and it is to the extent that they are adopted that they *open* [*ouvrent*] something, and that they *consist*; but this is equally true of all the words that we employ, each of which were, once upon a time, forged by a speaker, and which, each being as such a secondary retention belonging to a speaker of a language, have become collective secondary retentions, constituting *horizons of expectation common to a group*: they constitute as such, that is, again, as *elpis*, the pre-individual funds from which this group individuates itself socially as a *we*, but only *to the extent* that, in it, the *Is* psychically individuate themselves.

Now, such pre-individual funds are therefore woven of the expectations shaping and configuring secondary and collective retentions and, for this reason, we must pose that these funds are constituted by *collective secondary protentions*. As for these, they constitute masks, figures, occurrences and *supplementary* concretions, that is, *epiphylogenetics*, of what I will henceforth refer to as *archi-protentions*,[16] and that constitute the drive-based funds [*fonds pulsionnel*] of the epiphylogenetic living being, insofar as it constitutes a process of psycho-social individuation linked to the process of vital individuation proper to its biological root. Insofar as it permits the ortho-thetic stabilization of these collective secondary protentions, grammatization makes possible projections, each time original, of collective protentions, that is, of advances of individuation, and practices of *hypomnemata* inscribed in this register. But more generally, all epiphylogenetic practices have a projective aspect, through which they open new retentional and collective horizons. It is for this reason that Husserl could legitimately see in surveying and in the polishing of marble surfaces practices that, combined with hypomnesic practices for the notation of geometric reasoning, gave birth to the concepts of geometry.

Today, however, *the function of the culture and programming industries is to take control of these processes constituting collective secondary retentions. This control is achieved by replacing inherited pre-individual funds with what the culture and programming industries produce, and through this substitution to cause the adoption of retentional funds conceived according to the needs of marketing* – that is, to make every bit of collective secondary protention submit to the interests of investment. It does this at the risk of making totally inaccessible all consistent projections, that is, all protention of that which, precisely because it does not exist, consists, and confers to the existent its *motive*.

Hence the production and promotion of 'superficially sketched images', as Leroi-Gourhan puts it, and which, Rifkin adds, are collected in American malls as the totality 'of world culture [. . .] in the form of bits of entertainment to delight and amuse visitors and stimulate the desire to buy'. The problem is that such funds cannot form the object of symbolic participation for those who are thereby distracted from *their own* individuation (*distraction* means at the same time to separate, detach, subtract, divert and conceal, but also *dissuade or make renounce*), that is, for those who thereby lose their possibilities for individuating themselves, because they are internalizing the collective secondary retentions produced every day in production studios, in television studios, and in the *artificial living spaces* of reality television: produced and broadcast en masse by a hyper-synchronic broadcast system, aiming precisely to reduce the differences between primary selections, that is, to *intimately control the process* by homogenizing individual pasts, since these collective secondary retentions no longer constitute synchronic funds *adopted singularly* because *transmitted singularly*. They are produced and broadcast in a way that *short-circuits the entire process of transmission that the ascendants of a social group would otherwise take upon themselves,* a process constituted outside the programmes of the programme schedule itself. Targeted programme segmentation based on generational differences ends up completely suspending the authority of ascendants. The programmes of these programme industries never aim for the elevation of audiences, but on the contrary are always aiming at levelling and equalizing their audiences, including those generations who, though segmented, wear the same sneakers, gilded or otherwise. This is something of which the French have been aware at least since François Mitterrand privatized the public audiovisual industry without redefining its role, and since Valéry Giscard d'Estaing publicly revealed this privatization project at the same time as he revealed his talents as an accordionist:[17] levelling is always a question of lowering.

This is why these programmes are not forms of leisure at all. Leisure is essentially that which makes time free [*loisible*] for the one for whom it is leisure. Leisure is that through which someone is able to make time for themselves (thus, for example, Leibniz speaks of writing as permitting the 'examination of everything at leisure', the examination of the objects that it presents to us and that it produces – all those hypomneses supporting our anamneses), which is utterly to the contrary of these industrial temporal objects and of everything that accompanies them as derived products. Leisure, insofar as it is *otium*, cultivates the desire for individuation of the one who practises it, that is, the desire to raise themselves above themselves, and it is something that never consumes that which remains free – because consuming [*consommation*], like consumption [*consomption*], is an addiction.[18] This elevation constitutes the conquest of the individuation of this individual, as that which specifies *their own* singularity through the *experience* they have made of the *singularity of everything they encounter by and in their practices* of *otium*.

This is because the singularity of the secondary retentions of an individual is that which 'pro-tends' or 'pro-duces' his or her possibility of *encountering the singularity of that which happens to them*, and that concretizes itself as the singularity of primary selections that they effectuate at the moment of the experience of that which happens – that which happens being thus always an *accident* that comes to redistribute in turn the organization of secondary retentions acquired anteriorly.[19] For all that, however, what happens in this way only happens from out of the fund of collective secondary retentions which, as heritage, must be interpreted. In fact, the process of individuation, as primary selection, is always at the same time:

1. The interpretation of the event that happens.
2. The *re*-interpretation of the *past experience* of the individual to whom it happens, and that happens to them as an individual experience woven with secondary retentions.
3. The interpretation of the *funds of collective secondary retentions and protentions* that have been transmitted to the psychic individual as pre-individual milieu and within the collective individual, *via* the ascendants, parents, institutions, books, works and so on, by which is conquered, as elevation, the possibility of constituting a singular, individual experience: thus from language, which is learned and received from ascendants as collective secondary retentions forming a linguistic system.

But it is the same for all social behaviour. To walk is already to raise oneself in this sense, and there are styles of walking, gaits, that, as Marcel Mauss indicated, are already bodily techniques, that is, social facts. More generally, *everything that Bertrand Gille called the 'other systems', in order to designate social systems other than the technical system, are woven from such collective secondary retentions and protentions, themselves engrammed in the form of traces, of these materializations and spatializations of past time that I call tertiary retention,* and that forms the epiphylogenetic milieu, that is, the pre-individual milieu, of psychic and collective individuation.

These engrammes form *hypomnemata* as supports of cultivated practices, practices that in theological and aristocratic society remained the sole privilege of clerics, but that, in *democratic* society, must be systematically cultivated and, in particular, cultivated from the specific possibilities offered by the digital stage of the industrial development of grammatization.

7. *Otium* and *negotium*

Numerous domains of existence, in fact, *necessitate a constant, conjoined interpretation of collective and individual secondary retentions, and of the primary selections producing primary retention*, an interpretation often practised in relation to ancestors that one at times calls masters, and that constitute, as such, *practices* properly speaking, that is, *cultures* – ways of cultivating that which, because it has been raised, tends *spontaneously* to *fall back* into the everydayness [*ordinaire*] of things.

Singularity and that which *sustains* it as that which is raised, to be able to see from the shoulders of a giant and thereby achieve a longer and broader view, is what, departing from the ordinary, is in this sense literally extra-ordinary. And for this reason it must be ceaselessly protected, reaffirmed, and as such cultivated. This permanent care is expressed when a mother says to her child that it is not appropriate to put one's fingers in one's nose: this restraint, this reserve *transmitted* to the infant *body*, is *already* the *metron* that affirms the singularity of life as an existence that is not simply the satisfaction of bodily needs, but its elevation towards the desirable, lovable and cared-for body. The fact that this *metre* of behaviour, inculcating the notion that it is inappropriate to pick one's nose in front of others, is turned into elementary politeness, constituting within the *polis* the banality and everydayness [*ordinaire*] of existence, is the very thing that means there *is* an everydayness of existence itself, one which forgets that *bodily reserve* is as such extra-ordinary – and thus this is an *ordinariness* that is irreducible to subsistence behaviour. In order to *recall this fact, specific* practices are then cultivated that consist in interpretations of existence itself, and of the conditions of its elevation – and it is these that aim for consistences.

Otium is that which constitutes the practice of retentional systems through which collective secondary retentions are elaborated, selected and transmitted,[20] and through which, in turn, protentions are formed. The formation of these protentions always puts into play the singularity of the one who is taking aim with these protentions, since this process is always equally informed by the singularity of their secondary retentions, which are precisely *not* collective. Since some retentions and protentions are collective, however, then even though *otium* originally characterized the activities of the nobility, an *otium* of the people nevertheless remained, managed through the calendar as moments of synchrony, during which believers must cultivate their faith by practising their cult, and during which they must also, as it were, *gather* [*recueillir*] their diachrony from out of the heart of this synchrony.

These practices are always those of a support, of a mnemotechnics, of an instrument that supports a practical memory. It is, for example, the practices of the book, that is to say, of the Bible, or the practices of *hypomnemata* of the Epicureans, the Stoics, the Anchorites and the Cenobites, but it is also musical or poetic practice. All practice, insofar as it is *otium*, is sustained by tertiary retention – by secondary retentions objectivated and materialized, expressed in some material form, and that thus become transmissible, inheritable and adoptable, at the limit as bodily techniques, which are materializations in the flesh, something that is also true of the liturgy (which literally means *public service*) of the body of the faithful. This is the way in which the Church,

before being the opium of the people, was its *otium*, and constituted a *salvation* of souls insofar as it accorded them a day of *rest
giving access to questions of existence* and, through that, protect-
ing their existence: existence as elevation towards bringing into
question.

In fact, no society has ever existed that did not contain practices
comparable to what the Roman nobility called *otium*. No such
society exists, *except in the West of the industrial democracies*
which, taking themselves for post-industrial societies, are submitted to the 'leisure' industries, industries that are in fact the very
negation of leisure, that is, of *otium* as practice, since these industries are constituted through the hegemony of imperatives arising
from *negotium*. Such is their decadence.

Now, the technologies that sustain these industries, as mnemo-
technologies, whether analogue or digital, are tertiary retentions
that, like the alphabet of the nascent *polis*, support access to the
pre-individual funds of all psychic and collective individuation.
Tertiary retention exists in all human societies. It conditions individuation, as symbolic sharing [*partage*], which makes possible
the exteriorization of individual experience in epiphylogenetic
traces. When it becomes industrial, however, tertiary retention
constitutes technologies of control that fundamentally alter symbolic exchange: resting on the *opposition* of producers and consumers, these technologies make possible the hyper-synchronization
of calculated conscious time, and the decomposition of time itself,
that is, of individuation.

Consciousnesses and the bodies they inhabit as their behaviours
are therefore more and more woven by the same secondary retentions and tend to select the same primary retentions, and hence
to increasingly resemble one another: thus *branded*, they seem to
have little to say, finding themselves meeting less and less often,
and cast instead into their solitude in front of screens, where
they can devote less and less of their time to leisure – insofar
as leisure means time free of all the constraints dictated by
negotium.

But this does not mean that leisure time is free of all rule: on
the contrary, there is practice and culture because there is ancestry
and inherited obligations that, far from being the opposite of the
freedom of singular time, are, as pre-individual funds, the condi-

tion of such freedom. This is what forms itself as – and forms – consistences. These 'forms', which are however wholly informed by the material constraints of tertiary retention permitting their stabilization and transmission, metastabilize themselves in the course of forming themselves as a process of psychic and collective individuation, just as whirlpools morphogenetically maintain themselves within the current of a river drifting with variations of flow, temperature and so on – although it is also possible to direct the course of water into a turbine, which then creates a mechanical whirlpool, suppressing all those whirlpools that form merely from the operation of the laws of fluid mechanics. In certain cases, such fluvial adjustments can create serious environmental disorders. And yet they are rarely useless; they are nearly always necessary. We must compose. But we must not compose regardless of the price. We must at times oppose. And in order to preserve those whirlpools that are individual singularities, without which no individuation processes could occur, we must oppose more than ever.

8. Note on Hannah Arendt: *otium* and *vita activa*

The separation between *otium* and *negotium* that I try to define not as an opposition but as a distinction, a separation passing through the epochs of philosophical asceticism and religious asceticism, which constitute synchronizations of the psychic and collective individuation process, for example, as the *otium* of the people, and a separation that is maintained in every question about the difference between the activity of subsistence and activities of existence – this separation is close to what Hannah Arendt tried to rethink through the notion, itself also ancient, of *vita activa*, although I am unsure whether I fully understand her intentions. More important, however, is the fact that, on the one hand, Arendt showed very clearly the way in which this question is transformed throughout the course of the history of metaphysics, of the West and of monotheism, and the fact that, on the other hand, she has the praiseworthy audacity to try to propose her own redefinition of *vita activa*, with a gesture that is clearly quite close to what I myself want to outline here with the notion of *otium*.

Arendt's position is complex: she wanted to revisit the meaning of a term around which diverse conceptions of psycho-social individuation have stratified themselves. Even though Arendt relied on the analyses of Aristotle, who proposed in principle an absolute difference between the lives of those confined by their subsistence needs and those who are free from this confinement, that is, those who exist in a relation to that which is beautiful, whether this is the beauty lying within pleasure, or within the action in which political life consists, or within the contemplation of that which is and constitutes the *kosmos*, she nevertheless differed from Aristotle insofar as she integrated subsistence into this *vita activa*:

> With the term *vita activa*, I propose to designate three fundamental human activities: labour, work, and action.[21]

The problem here is that work – which, as the object that remains, constitutes the world as such – is according to Arendt completely foreign to action, which is

> the only activity that goes on directly between men without the intermediary of things or matter.[22]

And here, I believe, she ignored the role of tertiary retention and of grammatization, and, more generally, of epiphylogenesis as the condition of access to pre-individual funds without which there can be no action. The same problem arises when she says (and Jürgen Habermas will prolong this gesture):

> Wherever the relevance of speech is at stake, matters become political by definition, for speech is what makes man a political being.[23]

Now, if language is political, this is because it is a matter of epiphylogenesis, of which it is merely a modality. And, as well, it is the tertiary inscription of language that confers upon it its politicality, as for instance with the law to which one can refer because it has objectivated the time of discourse by spatializing it – in the form of *hypomnemata*.

The importance that Arendt accorded to birth and to the 'new-comer' amounts to the capacity for rupture lying within the process of psychic and collective individuation. Now, this is related to action properly speaking:

> [T]he newcomer possesses the capacity of beginning something anew, that is, of acting.[24]

As such, Arendt came to think much of what I call here the question of individuation, and in order to do so she tried to extract the original meaning of the term '*vita activa*', from the concretions in which it had become sedimented. She thus recalled that, even though within tradition this term fundamentally derives from the conflict between Socrates (representative of philosophy) and the city, it was also a translation into medieval Latin of Aristotle's '*bios politikos*'. For Augustine, the term:

> as *vita negotiosa* or *actuosa*, [. . .] still reflects its original meaning: a life devoted to public-political matters.[25]

But in this case, it would be a matter of actions the legitimacy of which derives only from their absolute difference from those actions necessitated by subsistence. As conceived since Aristotle, *vita activa* – as analogue of *bios politikos* – is not linked to anything, neither to labour nor to work: it is political life insofar as it is entirely free, and which in practice constitutes as such the leisure of the free man.

Now, this changes with Christianity, which opposes *vita activa* to *vita contemplativa*, the latter equivalent to *bios theoretikos*. *Vita contemplativa* then surpasses in value, beyond any measure, all existence, and hence, therefore, all activity, including political activity. It is in this way that *otium* comes to be opposed to *negotium*, understood as interest taken in public affairs in general. And yet, this is a matter of public interest, not private interest: as such, this is not *negotium* in the sense that we have already encountered, that is, as activity of subsistence, but precisely a modality of *otium* as the activity of existence in the city, which is precisely what Arendt was aiming for with her reinvention of the term *vita activa*.

Nevertheless, on the one hand, *otium* and *negotium* come from the Roman world of Epicureans and Stoics, well before primitive Christians, and, on the other hand, the opposition between contemplation and action comes, in the end, from Plato. And there, too, the superiority of contemplation leads to the suspension of all activity, including political activity: this is the *skhole*, which could translate the Latin *otium* as:

> freedom from political activity and not simply leisure time.[26]

By contrast, in Aristotle, the separation between rest and non-rest affects *all* forms of *bios* insofar as they are forms of *askholia*, of which rest would be a mode.[27] And, according to Thomas Aquinas reading Aristotle, these movements are in an essential relation to that unmoving which is the True: we will rediscover this problematic, which is also that of God as the prime unmoving mover, in the following chapter. In any case, *vita activa*:

> Up to the beginning of the modern age [. . .] never lost its negative connotation of 'un-quiet,' *nec-otium, a-skholia.*[28]

And finally, Arendt explained that she had to change the meaning of '*vita activa*' from the meaning conferred by tradition, to the degree, precisely, that this meaning depended on contemplation, on conceiving the elevation of life as consisting in nothing other than contemplation, whereas for her it was a matter of rethinking politics, that is, action, a matter of liberating action from the weight of metaphysics:

> Traditionally, therefore, the term *vita activa* receives its meaning from the *vita contemplativa* [. . .] the use of the term *vita activa*, as I propose it here, is in manifest contradiction to the tradition [. . .] the enormous weight of contemplation in the traditional hierarchy has blurred the distinctions and articulations within the *vita activa* itself.[29]

In fact, what I am myself trying to propose is that *otium*, insofar as it cannot be confounded with *negotium* (to which, nevertheless, as its name indicates, it seems to be opposed, or rather, which seems, by its name, to be opposed to it), on the one hand, cannot simply be opposed to *negotium* – the opposition between them being precisely the metaphysical attitude that it is a matter of abandoning – and yet, on the other hand, comprises an *activity*, which can be entirely collective, on the condition that it is devoted to existence insofar it is free in relation to its own subsistence, that is, exceeds subsistence by exceeding itself, by projecting the consistences that move it, 'motivate' it, *form the reasons to act*, which themselves constitute the excess or surplus [*excé-dent*] of general economy, as Bataille claimed. As spirit and consistence, these reasons extend beyond the surplus of resources issuing from the accumulation of capital, which, however, is its condition – this capitalizable surplus being necessary in order to be freed from the immediate pressure of subsistence and hence in order to be capable of encountering the excess as what is incalculable, improbable, and inexistent yet consistent. In other words, capital and its calculation as accumulation are needed in order that what surpasses these as the experience of the incalculable can arise, that experience of the incalculable that I here call 'singularity' insofar as existence is only conferred as the experience of a consistence.

And it is here that we encounter the limit of Arendt's approach, an approach that amounts to the privilege she *gave* to the action and thought of the *vita activa*, or of what I myself call existence, since it is the reason to act: Arendt failed to locate the irreducible place, in this action, of *tekhnè*; and, at the same time, she remained completely blind to the question of grammatization. For the same reason, she conferred to immortality a place against the eternal that she believed could be found in *vita contemplativa*, because she confused immortality and *kleos*.

In any case *otium*, as I have here defined it, is not simply the 'contemplative' life: as with what Arendt attempted to think, it is a matter of a practice, that is, an activity, which may be public. In brief, it is a matter of that which, like discipline, enables the raising of existences capable of considering consistences, and this is something that can and must be produced in an entirely practical way. As for the question of *kleos*, which must not be confused with immortality, Arendt referred this, as glory, to the fame of the exceptional.

9.   The culture of the exception as rule

Through the *industrial expropriation of mnemo-technologies*, that is, through retentional systems that are the technical supports required by all psychic and collective individuation, the twentieth century optimized the conditions of production and consumption by linking them tightly together. This was achieved by controlling the time devoted both to work and to non-work, through the deployment of calculation and information technologies in order to control production and investment, and through communication technologies used to control consumption and social behaviour, including political behaviour. These two spheres are today integrated and constitute a form of global control, within which existence is totally submitted to models of consumption, themselves totally conforming to the necessities of production, that is, of subsistence, of *negotium*.

Now, this submission is structurally antagonistic to all *otium*, to all cultural *practices*, for which the hegemony of *negotium* substitutes 'usages', defining themselves as models of consumption.

With digitalization, the great delusion and trap is, however, no longer just the notion of the 'leisure society', that epoch postulated by the post-industrial fable, but also the 'personalization' of individual needs. Félix Guattari speaks of the production of 'dividuals', that is, the particularization of singularities, their absorption into the totality as mere parts, through their submission to computational cognitive technologies, which constitute the optimal technological model of control societies. Through *user profiling* and other novel control methods, these cognitive technologies permit a subtle use of conditioning, referring here to Pavlov as much as to Freud. Hence those services that incite readers of a book to read other books read by other readers of those books. Or, again, search engines that increase the value of the most consulted references, reinforcing at a stroke their consultation, and constituting an extremely refined ratings system.

These digital machines, directing the production processes of machines programmed by remote control in flexible workshops (industrial robotics having become essentially a mnemo-technology of production), are also the same machines that, when put at the service of marketing, and according to the same *norms and stan-*

dards, organize consumption. Contrary to what Benjamin believed, this is not a matter of a deployment of 'mass narcissism', but, on the contrary, it is the massive destruction of individual and collective narcissism through the constitution of hyper-masses. As the *perfect fulfilment of nihilism*, this generalized herdishness induced by the elimination of primordial narcissism is the *effective liquidation of exceptionality* [*de l'exception*].

In place of collective imaginaries and individual histories tied to the heart of the psychic and collective individuation process, industrial temporal objects substitute mass standards that tend to reduce the singularity of individual practices and to reduce their exceptional character. Now, *the exception is the rule*, but a rule that is never formulable: it lives only through the occurrence of an irregularity, that is, it is not formalizable and calculable by a rule-driven descriptive apparatus that would be applicable in every case, each case constituting the different occurrences of this *rule by default*.

Hence, there may indeed be something common to all the poems of a single poet. But this common membership can never be reduced to a mere generative algorithm. Because with each new poem, the poet individuates himself or herself: he or she becomes – he or she becomes otherwise than a mere descriptive algorithm. A poet is individuation par excellence, insofar as, being essentially inscriptive, the poet is not describable – which is what also constitutes the performative character of poetry, and, more generally, of the idiom: what is true of the poet is true of the idiom in general.

It is thus that the exception is the rule of the *excess* – and of its counterpart, the *lack* [*défaut*]: it is as such a rule that *exceeds every rule*, a *rule by default*. This is why, for a long time, it was referred to God, who constitutes *absolutely irregularity as the rule of the incomparability of singularities* – as absolute past and absolute future, that is, as a past that has never been present, and a future that will never be present, and, as such, and very paradoxically, let's say *extra-ordinarily*, as a *presence incomparable to whatever present there may be*.

The exception is the rule, but it must be cultivated – that is, by the cult, or by culture as *otium* – at once to *contain* the excess within it, and to reaffirm and to ceaselessly *maintain* it, because it is structurally lacking [*fait structurellement défaut*], and appeared in the first place as (de)fault, that is, as the *singularity of an idiocy*. Being turned to the extra-ordinary towards which it raises itself, the exception is contested and denied by the *stupid* [*bête*] but *spontaneous* force of the everyday [*ordinaire*]. As rule, the excess that is the exception is life as will to power, as force that must be protected from that counter-force that is nothing other than the will to power turned back on itself, the *spontaneously strong banality* of everydayness, tending spontaneously to submit existence to the hegemony of subsistence.

Voluntary or spontaneous, this *power* or *potential* is what must be both *contained and maintained as the best and the worst* – by cultivating its *act*.

The extra-ordinary towards which the exception is turned is consistence. An exception always aims towards a consistence, towards something that does not exist and that, as such, is not everyday, that exceeds what exists, and, *a fortiori*, exceeds that which subsists. All existence cultivates knowledge of an ex-ception that bears it and through which it ex-sists, and all forms of singularity are always such exceptions, as humble and invisible as they may remain in the eyes of the ordinary mortals [*commun*] that we are, and, in this sense, they are detours that existence takes in turning towards that which consists. The consistent, which is not ordinary, is raised and, as such, puts singularities *into movement*, that is, *e-motivates* [*é-meut*] them – but as that which moves them *towards themselves* insofar as they *become*. Now, they can, in this becoming, either regress or, on the contrary, raise themselves. When they raise themselves, the becoming becomes a future [*le devenir devient un advenir*]: then the singularities *advene* [*adviennent*]. This is what Bousquet or Deleuze call, after the Stoics, an *event*.

These singularities must, although they advene, be maintained as well as contained, and this is called cultivating them. Now, the goal of marketing is to make these singularities comparable and categorizable by transforming them into empty particularities that can be 'regulated' by capturing and harnessing libidinal energy, in a way that is both hyper-massified and hyper-segmented. It is a matter, at bottom, of a capitalist economy that has become fundamentally *anti*-libidinal and, as such, self-destructive.

Capitalism could only pursue its development *in peace* by sustaining desire, that is, by articulating the play of drives as that *composition* that is desire. Now, only that which is singular, and to that extent exceptional, is desirable: I only desire what to me seems exceptional; there is no desire for banality, but there is a repetition compulsion that *tends* towards banality – and that the *psyche*, within which Eros and Thanatos are composed, originarily harbours. The culture industry and marketing thus try to develop the desire to consume but, when consumption becomes nothing other than the ordeal of pure banality, it deceives and frustrates desire, *kills* desire, because it reinforces the death-drive: instead of sustaining desire, the culture industry and marketing provoke and exploit the repetition compulsion. They in this way thwart the life-drive. And because desire is essential to consumption, this process is self-destructive. Such is the manner in which Monsieur Le Lay digs capitalism's grave.

I can only desire the singularity of some thing to the extent that this thing is the mirror of a singularity that I am, of what I don't yet know, and that this thing reveals to me. But, to the extent that capital must hyper-massify behaviour, it must also hyper-massify desire and herd individuals together. At this point, the exception becomes that which must be combated: such is the advent of nihilism, industrial democracy engendering this herd society that now finds itself close to the abyss.

10.   The political economy of singularities

This is a genuine *aporia of industrial political economy*, and it leads sooner or later to war. Now, this war is impossible: it would not only be the Third World War, but the last, and even the end of humanity. A jumpstart [*sursaut*] is therefore required. This jumpstart could only be a politics both industrial and cultural, which I have previously named a political economy of the spirit, necessitated by the advent of technologies of the spirit. But it must be just as much a political economy of singularities, that is, of the *exception* insofar as it must be *cultivated*: at the same time and ceaselessly *maintained* and *contained* as that which is spontaneously lacking [*défaut*], even though life *wills* the exception and is nothing other than this *will* – but this life, as existence, is that which the hegemony of *negotium* tends to suffocate.

What in France one calls the 'cultural exception' is the cloak concealing the depth of these questions. However indispensable the measures it entails may be, it has been instrumentalized as a pure and simple political slogan. And it prevents those who lay their hands on this slogan from reflecting on the exception in general, and from taking the measure of the questions posed by the deployment of hyper-industrial society, by the becoming-cultural of capitalism that it signifies, and by the generalized proletarianization and the symbolic misery in which it results. From this primordial question for the becoming of global society, such cant causes a secondary problem, that is regional and sectorial, indeed 'corporative', and downplays the cultural question just as much as do the ultraliberal arguments that, opposing all 'cultural exception' measures, and within the framework of international commercial accords, attempt to liquidate everything exceptional.

The question of culture, such as I have tried to re-elaborate it here, is seemingly overshadowed by these two positions, as antagonistic as they may appear, and which dissimulate the fact that an historic mutation of capitalism has occurred, through which a tendency to *totalize* existence has been cultivated, that is, a tendency to reduce existence to subsistence. This is the result of the hegemonic growth of the tendency towards the levelling of all things characteristic of fulfilled nihilism. And because it constitutes a major obstacle in the pursuit of national, continental, and global psychic and collective individuations, it calls for the invention of a political economy of singularities that does not oppose the process of grammatization of which capitalism is an epoch, but on the contrary reinvents the composition of forces that, alone, can confer a future upon this becoming.

This question is not limited to the life of what one calls 'culture', that occupies, for example, in France, the minister designated by this very name: every aspect of everyday existence is submitted to the hyper-industrial conditioning of ways of everyday life. This is the most disturbing problem of industrial ecology imaginable: the mental, intellectual, affective and aesthetic capacities of humanity are massively threatened, at the very moment that human groups have at their disposal unprecedented means of destruction.

The disbanding [*débandade*] in which this ruin of the libido consists is also political, to the extent that politicians adopt marketing techniques to transform themselves into products, from playing the accordion on television, to the delegation of their political programmes to advertising agencies, as was the case for the presidential campaigns of François Mitterrand and for recent European elections. The inevitable result is that these pretenders to being the people's representatives discredit themselves in the eyes of the people, who, no longer respecting them, allow themselves to make a suicidal vote (and not only as a protest vote) or to abstain from voting: voters feel about politicians and their apparatuses the same disgust they have for every other product. The end result is the French election of 28 March 2004, where the electorate voted against the government, but not for a party that had any programme; and it is as well the character of the European electorate that largely abstained on 13 June of the same year, both these electorates suffering from a general destruction of libidinal economy and from a political desire that was no longer able to find any satisfaction: *philia*, with which Aristotle defined the relation between citizens, is a highly refined and patiently *cultivated* fruit of the libidinal economy.

From 21 April 2002 to 13 June 2004 successive injunctions were addressed to the political class to combat the symbolic and psychological misery that inevitably also becomes *political misery*. And it is not by chance if the political debacle of the French government, in the course of regional elections on 28 March 2004, was crystallized around questions linked to culture and research. The cultural question is not politically trivial: it is the very heart of politics, including beyond the current context that 'cultural capitalism' constitutes. Because culture is also libido, and the *city* is a *specific* mode of the libidinal economy characterizing *all* human society. But in the current context, within which industrial activity tries essentially to capture and harness libidinal energy, the articulation between culture and economy must become the heart of the political question – and must do so *at the European level*. Politics must before anything else be cultural, but in a profoundly renewed sense: not in the sense according to which a minister of culture, or a European parliamentary commission, serves or fails to serve diverse and varied clientele of the cultural arts – for instance, casual employees [*intermittents*] within the programme industries – but rather as a critique of the limits of a hyper-industrial capitalism that has become destructive of the social organizations in which processes of psychic and collective individuation consist.

4

Wanting to Believe
In the Hands of the Intellect

Because the desirable is a motor and, if thought is in its turn a motor, this is because it finds the principle of its movement in the desirable.

Aristotle[1]

Instead of having recourse to the concepts that habitually serve to distinguish man from other living beings (instinct and intelligence, absence or presence of speech, of society, of economy, etc. etc.), the notion of *program* is invoked. It must of course be understood in the cybernetic sense, but cybernetics is itself intelligible only in terms of a history of the possibilities of the trace as the unity of a double movement of protention and retention. This movement goes far beyond the possibilities of the 'intentional consciousness'. [. . .] If the expression ventured by Leroi-Gourhan is accepted, one could speak of a 'liberation of memory', of an exteriorization always already begun but always larger than the trace which, beginning from the elementary programs of so-called 'instinctive' behavior up to the constitution of electronic card-indexes and reading machines, enlarges *différance* and the possibility of putting in reserve: it at once and in the same movement constitutes and effaces so-called conscious subjectivity, its logos, and its theological attributes.

Jacques Derrida[2]

It is a question of attaining this will that the event creates in us; of becoming the quasi-cause of what is produced within us, the Operator; of producing surfaces and linings in which the event is

reflected, finds itself again as incorporeal and manifests in us the
neutral splendour which it possesses in itself in its impersonal and
pre-individual nature.

Gilles Deleuze[3]

1. The law of regression: being only intermittently

Wanting to believe. Such is my title.[4] And it has a subtitle: *In the
hands of the intellect.* I am thus playing on the two possible mean-
ings of this subtitle:

- In some way, it would be necessary to want to *believe in the
  hands* of the intellect, in the fact that the intellect has some
  hands, that it has always had them, and that this will endure,
  that it will still and always have hands, that nothing has yet
  been lost – because having hands, *here*, means *being able to do*
  something; as such, I would also have been able to change my
  title: *Wanting to believe and being able to do* [*faire*].
- But *Wanting to believe. In the hands of the intellect*, this also
  says that even when one is in the hands of the intellect, *in the
  grip* of the intellect, *imprisoned* in the intellect, between its
  hands – as one says in French, 'being in the hands of the police',
  that is, being *arrested* by the police, and, as such, *powerless* – it
  is necessary to *continue* to believe, it is necessary to *want* to
  believe.

In brief, it is a matter of *thinking the relation between the will
and the hand, such that they are believers. That is, also, intellectuals.* But here, instead of the intellect, let us rather speak of νουσ:[5]
this Greek word that defines that soul called *noetic* in Aristotle's
treatise, *On the Soul.* I will therefore speak to you of νουσ such
as it constitutes, for Aristotle, the noetic soul, but in an *insurmountable relation to the sensitive soul.*

I am speaking here in the context of what I have called hyper-
industrial society, where the singularly perceptible [*sensible*], as
object of an aesthetic *experience* of singularity consisting in an
enlargement of sense, is replaced by an archaistic and *regressive
conditioning* of sensibility.[6] Now, from where does the *possibility*
of this regression derive?

Sensibility or perceptibility, thought as such for the first time by Aristotle, characterizes *two types of 'souls'*: the sensitive soul and the noetic soul. More generally, Aristotle distinguishes three types of souls, that is, of being which find within themselves their movement, their auto-mobility, their animation: the vegetative soul, the sensitive soul and the noetic soul. The sensitive soul inherits the 'vegativity' of the vegetative soul, and the noetic soul inherits the sensitivity of the sensitive soul (and through this, it equally contains the vegetavity of the vegetative soul). But the sensitivity of the noetic soul is noetic *through and through*, trans-formed by the fact that it is a sensitivity *of the noetic*: it is the *power* of the noetic, and that it is noetic means that it is inscribed in *logic* – the noetic sensible opens on to sense as *semiosis*, and not only as *aesthesis*. 'Logic' does not mean, then, conforming to rules of rationality but means, rather, inscribed within a *becoming-symbolic*. All sensibility in act becomes, for a noetic soul, the support of an *expression*. This expression (discernment, *krinein*, judgement, *making-a-difference*[7]) is a *logos* – word or gesture: narration, poem, music, engraving, representation in all its forms, but also *savoir-faire and savoir-vivre in general*. This is not how metaphysics understands *logos*, but it is how it must be understood, in particular within the horizon of the question of political economy, which is that of my intervention here today.

This becoming-symbolic as *logos*, which only is in the course of its being ex-pressed, is what I call an *ex-clamation*: the *noetic* experience of the sensible is *exclamatory*. It exclaims itself before the sensible insofar as it is *sensational*, that is, experience of a *singularity* that is *incommensurable*, and *always in excess*. The exclamatory soul, that is, sensational and not only sensitive, *enlarges* its sense by exclaiming it symbolically.

However, the becoming-symbolic of the noetic sensible in the exclamation of the sensational can become the logistico-symbolic *control* exerted by the noetico-aesthetic technologies, which are the technologies of information and communication, and the sensational can thus turn bad. This is what happens when conditioning is substituted for experience. The exclamation is then that of the 'sensationalist press'. It is a regression towards the reactive and herdish behaviour of sensitive souls, where the sensational engenders the panic behaviour of crowds. But this is not a perversion caused by the culture industries or by what is now called cultural capitalism: it is inscribed in the structure of the noetic *psyche*. Aristotle emphasizes, in fact, that the noetic soul is not always in action: its mode of being *ordinary* is to be simply sensitive, which means that it remains in the stage of inert power, of its *powerless power*. It is only intermittently that it passes to the sensational stage of the noetic, which is also its extra-ordinary stage. Heidegger, commenting on the *Nicomachean Ethics*, writes that:

> Man cannot constantly dwell among the *timiotata*; for man, this autonomous mode of Being, forever attending to the *timiotata*, is unthinkable.[8]

And in *Metaphysics* Book A, Aristotle cites Simonides:

> God alone may have this prerogative.[9]

That is to say, the privilege of always being in action [*en acte*]. The beastly or stupid tendency that was already thought in Aristotle as the regression of the intellective-sensational soul to the sensitive stage, is what contemporary industrial entropy exploits – *just as* it exploits the projective and fascinating capacity of the cinema of consciousness, the originarily cinemato-graphic structure of 'consciousness', the fact that consciousness has the character of an 'archi-cinema'.[10]

The noetic soul cannot therefore be simply opposed to the sensitive soul, from which it must on the other hand nevertheless be distinguished, as Aristotle did in fact do. The sensitive and the noetic compose as potential and act. The sensitive soul, according to Hegel, is the *dunamis* of the noetic soul that is only ever in action (*energeia, entelecheia*) intermittently. This would mean that as a general rule – and putting it vulgarly, or stupidly – the noetic soul is stupid [*bête*]. Indeed, nasty [*méchante*]. And nothing is perhaps more stupid or nasty than wanting to ignore this – that is, wanting to ignore that this applies *first of all* to the one pro-claiming it, and does so *as the insurmountable limit of this state-ment itself*.

One cannot *oppose* the sensitive soul *in action* to the noetic soul *in potential* because it is matter of a *process* within which *all of this composes*. Thought processually, *dunamis* and *entelecheia* are no longer the equivalents of *hyle* and *morphe*, as metaphysics has generally presumed, but rather of what Simondon calls the *pre-individual* and the *quantum leap* as the act of an individuation process, as fulfilment of this individuation, where this 'fulfilment' ['*accomplissement*'] is nevertheless always the exteriorization of its incompletion [*inachèvement*], or in other words is always deficient [*par défaut*] *to the extent* that one *only ever is* intermittently – to the extent that one is irreducibly stupid [*bête*].

The (de)fault of origin is therefore also the origin of stupidity. This stupidity, insofar as it nevertheless gives this act, is that which can nevertheless also give *the idiocy of the idiom, that is, of singularity*. And this process is a circuit: a circuit of desire, where this desire is always an exclamation – the passage to the act in which noesis consists is as such and primordially an 'exteriorization'. I will speak of this exteriorization, but I lack the time to return to the circuit of desire.[11]

From the moment that noesis is primordially 'exteriorization', it is impossible to oppose the interior to the exterior, which is why I place this within quotation marks. This *distinction that does not oppose* – of which the cost and benefit is that the intellective can no longer be opposed to the sensible, that *logos* can no longer be opposed to hands – gives place to a difference, to a place or *khora* as that which opens this difference, and within which the forces of a process compose (and this is what metaphysics has failed to realize) as distinction and composition, *doing* and thinking.

The *Wirklichkeit* of this lack of *savoir-faire* is the rejection of technics as a process of ontological purification and, with technics, the rejection of fiction as condemned to being on the side of *pseudos*. But it is also the deployment of generalized proletarianization, which characterizes current capitalism.

One could not, therefore, strictly oppose the sensitive to the noetic, because the sensitive would be the potential of the noetic, or, as Hegel says, its *in itself*, such that *dunamis* here resembles matter. But, on the other hand, one cannot say that sensitivity as the *potential of the noetic* is the same thing as sensitivity as the *act of a soul of which the potential is then vegetative* – I therefore wish to speak of the sensitivity of the sensitive soul. But as one can no longer say that noeticity opposes sensitivity, or *aestheticity* (as when the intelligible is opposed to the sensible), we must conclude that insofar as action belongs to *aesthesis*, *nous* is itself aesthetic, but in an elevated sense, in some way lifted up by *nous* – by *nous* as the *power and action of exclamation*. That is to say, as belief. As, for example, when one says: *what beauty!* One *believes* then that it is beautiful – and without wanting to, without needing to want to, without even being able to want to, if not indeed according to a power that is, precisely, that of a *dunamis*.

An interpretative error must be avoided that would consist in posing that the sensitive soul is the animalian foundation of the noetic soul, which, endowed with a supplementary *logos*, would supplement the soul, or give spirit to the animal's soul. This error of reading consists in taking to the letter the definition of the soul as *zoon politikon*, as social animal, rational animal, speaking animal and so on. To avoid this error, or, in other words, to make the *aestheticity* of the noetic soul its very noeticity, rather than treating this as merely its matter, to which the intellect as its form would then confer its essence, I call the noetic soul 'sensational', the sensational as *experience* being then the act of *nous* and at the same time that of *logos*. And I further propose that *dunamis* cannot be thought according to the hylemorphic schema: it already carries within it, as pre-individual milieu, the *potential* to act – which, when it is intermittently produced, is its *knowledge*. Now, this knowledge is also, in Aristotle, the movement that produces *theos*, the first immobile mover, habitually translated as God, and to which each type of soul is, in its action, in a relation. From this point of view, the immobile mover is the moveability of all souls. One must then also say: their reason.

But we must also understand that the sensitive *potential* of the noetic act can equally be, at its limit, the very *impotential* of the noetic: such is the law of regression, or of unreason, inscribed in these souls that *are only . . . intermittently*, and that all tend to decay, according to the mode of their impotential potential, that is, their potential *incapability of passing into action*.

This regression and impotentiality or incapacity, the debility in which it consists, is the ordinary and quotidian fate of the noetic soul and its *care* [*souci*], that of which it must *take care*, which in this sense requires what I call a belief: the noetic soul, *between* these intermittences, where it passes to the act, loses sight of what *moves* it insofar as it is *noetic*, that is, sensational, namely, the *theos* that e-motes it in the sense of putting it in motion, motivating it as *giving and giving back reason* [*donner et rendre raison*]. Giving *and* giving back, because it gives a gift and a counter-gift – what I call a circuit.

In short, we are at the scene of what it would be necessary to call here the onto-theologico-political. And we are going to try to replay this scene, but in a new setting. Because Aristotle obviously did not read it himself as I propose to read it here. But this is only to the extent that Aristotle can – since the inadequation of his text, insofar as it is a text, that is, a fiction and, just as much, a *dunamis*, a potential, brings forth [*porte*] – constitute a pre-individual milieu of individuation that, transmitting what Simondon called a phase difference [*déphasage*] in the psycho-social individuation of the West, can intermittently leap beyond the *metaphysical* individuation that the West will have been – a West that is achieved, that is, finished, dead, given that capitalism fulfils itself as the advent of nihilism. And where Aristotelianism poses the *question of motor* in terms of causalities (material, formal, efficient and final), we must henceforth reason in terms of accidentality and automobility – that is, in terms of supplementarities: grammatologically, and in the sense according to which the supplement constitutes the *process* of a grammatization.

2. 'Acceding – if possible, inasmuch as it is possible – to another experience of singularity'

Having said all this, I would like to make clear that this lecture is a commentary on several phrases expressed orally by Jacques Derrida in 1994, in the course of a conversation between us that was intended for television broadcast, although this never eventuated, but which has since been published under the title *Echographies: Of Television*.[12] Jacques Derrida said the following – which he therefore did not originally write, although he reviewed the literary version transcribed from the videorecording:

Once 'democratization' or what we call by this name has, thanks
precisely to the technologies we were just now talking about, made
such 'progress' (I am putting all these words in quotes), to the point
where, the classical totalitarian ideologies having foundered, in
particular those that were represented by the Soviet world, the
neoliberal ideology of the market is no longer able to cope with its
own power – once this has happened, there is a clearer field for
this form of homecoming called 'petty nationalism,' the nationalism of minorities, regional or provincial nationalism, and for religious fundamentalism, which often goes with it [and which also
tries to reconstitute states]. Hence the *'regression'* which accompanies the acceleration of the technological process, which is always
also a process of delocalization – and which in truth follows it like
its shadow, practically getting confused with it. Here again, because
we are talking about a *double or polar movement*, there can be no
question, it seems to me, of choosing between the two, or of saying:
What matters is the acceleration of the technological process at the
expense of the desire for idiom or for national singularity. *Between
these two poles one must find, through negotiation, a way precisely
not to put the brakes on knowledge, technics, science, or research,
and to accede – if possible, inasmuch as it is possible – to another
experience of singularity, of idiom, one that is other*, that is not
bound up with these old phantasmatics called nationalism or with
a certain nationalist relationship to language, to singularity, to territory, to blood, to the old model of the borders of a nation-state.
I *would like* to think that the desire for singularity, and even the
desire or longing for home, without which, in effect, there is no
door nor any hospitality [. . .] I *would like to believe* that this
unconditional desire, which it is *impossible to renounce*, which
should not be renounced, is not tied in a necessary way to these
schema or watchwords called nationalism, fundamentalism, or
even to a *certain concept* of idiom or language . . .

I would like therefore to believe that this desire for singularity
can have another relation – it is very difficult – to technics, to
universality, to a certain uniformization of technics.[13]

Much could be said about this text, which began as an oral conversation. I will return to it in more detail elsewhere. I will here
only evoke *two* aspects of this text: on the one hand, the *polar*
articulation between technological development and *intensification* or, on the contrary, *the liquidation* of *singularity*; on the other

hand, and this will be my principal theme, the question of a *necessity of wanting to believe*, expressed in the conditional, but of conditionally believing in the unconditional (in 'this unconditional desire'), which is also the question of *belief as will*. Now, in this will as believing is equally posed the question of *fiction* – but I will say: of fiction *as operation*. And of operation *as political performance*. And this will of believing *as fiction*, and the *fashioning* [*facture*] of this fiction, such that it is always in some way a *manufacture*, is also the question of a *power* to believe, of a *power* to fiction, of a *power* of fiction, of a *potential* that *conditions a will*, but also of an *impotential* that, as *regression*, can provoke this fiction.

It is a matter here of '*unconditional* desire, which it is *impossible to renounce*'. But how does this 'renunciation' relate, *on this point*, to desire insofar as it is unconditional, that is, insofar as it *must not be* renounced, must not be ceded? And, furthermore, what is it that we want here to state should not be renounced? Is it a purely intellectual will (but what *is* a purely intellectual will?), or does it concern a struggle, a combat to lead, eventually in appealing to a force, to this force without which there is no law, but also to this force that could oppose itself to the law, to a force beyond-the-law that would want (why not?) to *reinvent* the law, *remake* the law? But what would then be the law of such a force, from where would such a law come, and who would impose it?

Because, after all, the law is made: it does not fall from the sky of ideas. There is no a priori form that would give shape to some kind of material fallen in advance like a turd. The passage to the act is not natural – unlike in the Platonic fable.

Renunciation sounds like a kind of grieving, that of metaphysics. This grieving is also what we have had to learn to 'negotiate':

> Between these two poles one must find, through negotiation, a way precisely not to put the brakes on knowledge, technics, science, or research, and *to accede – if possible, inasmuch as it is possible –* to *another experience* of singularity.[14]

That is to say that one must *compose*, one must *surpass the oppositions* that characterize metaphysics in all its epochs.

That one must compose also means that one must know how to renounce – that which, as the play of oppositions, constituted the *delusions and lures* of metaphysics, the *consolatory fates* and *compensatory behaviours* in which it has consisted. But also the *system of domination* of a certain *idea of the law*, according to which it would have fallen from the sky.

One must therefore renounce metaphysics in *all* these senses, but the entire issue is, however, for all that, to not renounce life, that is, a form of *struggle* – because then there would no longer be composition, but, precisely, a *de-composition*. Here, the question that is posed is then the necessity of *opposing* in order to save the possibility of composition, that is, also, to not purely and simply sink into what Nietzsche called nihilism. The question that imposes itself today is that of a *struggle for what it is impossible to renounce*, for that for which one must struggle, even if this means that one must *oppose oneself*. But it is a matter of not opposing oneself *reactively*. And *therefore*, in order to move forward, that is, not reactively, it is necessary to cast a 'glance at the current world'[15] and at its genealogy, and to practise what I call, after Jacques Derrida, a *history of supplements*.

But before moving on, I will append a question, which I only mention in passing even though it clearly constitutes one of the central stakes at issue here: when Jacques Derrida appeals to a negotiation that knows how to accede *both* to knowledge and to singularity, and that would do so, precisely –

if possible, inasmuch as it is possible

– is there not a problem? Why not pose in advance – and as the power of a *passage to the act* that only ever occurs intermittently, and that, of course, might therefore *never* occur – why not pose *in principle* what would be, for example, the principle of a political economy understood as a will to believe: that the development of the technological process *must be* the development of singularity, which it would have been, for instance, when it was a matter of the grammatization of the letter? This grammatization of the letter certainly came at a cost, at the cost of deficits, defaults, linguicides, idiocides, in particular in Latin America and Brazil, in the war of *spirits* that accompanies that of bodies,[16] and at the cost of an enormous stupidity, including and in particular what is named metaphysics, but it would certainly also be a matter of spirit, of that spirit about which Valéry writes, let us recall:

> A world transformed by spirit no longer presents to the mind the same perspectives and directions as before; it poses *entirely* new problems and countless *enigmas*.[17]

3. The system of supplements and its potential for individuation

Is it not on the condition of posing this principle as unconditional, while placing in suspense this *would-be* [or, this 'perhaps', *peut-être*] that constitutes the question of the intermittence of the access to *timiotata*, holding it, in other words, *in the conditions of improbability* in which alone belief can *consist*, this consistence being then its *power*, is it not on this condition without condition that one *can want to believe*? And *to believe in the hands* of the intellect, even when, as here, it is a question of *books in the hands* of the intellect?

Singularity is *constituted* through grammatization. I call grammatization the history of supplements that, in its orthothetic stage, opens the question of 'its' *as such* and closes off, as metaphysics, the interrogation of hypomnesis, yet while pursuing and intensifying its hypomnesic development, precisely as the history of the three technological revolutions of grammatization, within which must be included the reproduction of movement in all its forms. The unfurling of the *process* of grammatization, thus understood, constitutes the *Western history* of the supplement. This process, which Sylvain Auroux does not himself analyse *as* a process, is one part of the process of technical, psychic and collective individuation, where the *I*, the *we*, and the supplement (what I have elsewhere called the *it*) co-individuate themselves, thereby forming a *system of supplements*: *the* supplement is always already supplements. Grammatization is that which, in the individuation of the *system of* supplements, which *is* the history of supplements, concerns this *specific* dimension of supplementarity that is properly speaking hypomnesic. But this hypomnesic dimension of grammatization is not limited to symbolic utterances: it includes all the movements of the noetic soul, that it supports as *tekhné* in general – but that it only properly speaking discretizes, and only grammatizes in this sense, when the machine permits the reproduction of its gestures.

Hence grammatization does not only affect those utterances and symbolizations that are usually recognized as belonging to the domain of logic and intellect, of *nous* such as it has been thought by metaphysics, but equally affects the sensible or perceptible, such as the world of art enlarges it, but also, and especially, the *ars* in general, that is, the mechanical as well as the liberal arts, and, in other words, all *knowledge*, whether *theoretical* knowledge or *practical* knowledge, the latter consisting of *savoir-faire* and *savoir-vivre*. From out of this takes place what Marx described as the *reckoning [comput]* of the gestures of workers who, finding their knowledge formalized and exteriorized in the machine and, as such, grammatized, find themselves reduced to the condition of the proletariat. Such is the process of proletarianization, the accomplishment of industrial capitalism, carrying forward the process of grammatization and constituting the final epoch of the Western history of the supplement. From here, too, an analysis of the history of the supplement today, which can only be today a political task, must also be an analysis of the generalization of proletarianization.

Now, as for the future possibilities contained in this becoming in which grammatization as proletarianization consists, one must never stop repeating that the history of grammatization has always at the same time been an expropriation of the proper, that is, of that which, in the idiom, constitutes its idiomatic difference, and the possibility of replaying this difference in order to intensify it. This is what happens with the letter insofar as it leads to literature, as well as to the law and to the possibility of citizenship as a singularity posed *in law* (if not in fact – such is the *necessary, legal and legitimate fiction* of the law) for all citizens. And, beside this *difference between the fact and right of citizenship*, one could also speak of citizenship in potential and in act, and of *fiction and its law* held within this difference, and within the intermittences that it handles, and within the *belief* that it calls forth.

This intensification of difference within grammatization in which consists the nascent *polis* is what I have analysed, in relation to the literal orthothesis that orthographic writing constitutes, as the production of *différantial* identification. The *polis*, insofar as it is an epoch of grammatization and, more precisely, insofar as it is a translation into the social organization of movement of the development of hypomneses through the epiphylogenetic becoming produced in the Mediterranean basin (and which I will show elsewhere must be placed in relation to the economy, commerce and subsistence activities in general, thus in relation to technics in general, including art[18]), is equally the appearance of education (the citizen must be literate), such that this is no longer simply initiation: it is the *grammatist*, the master of letters, who in the form of the sage replaces the priest or the mage, and who is thus also the origin of the sophist as well as of philosophy as academy (which Plato wants to make a school of philosophers conceived as the only legitimate rulers of the city) and school. Now, the school as the hearth within which citizens are forged consists, as a republican and demo-cratic institution, in spreading access to the *timiotata* while *instituting* this access – which is also to organize *eris* as elevation towards the *ariston*.

From this arises the question that imposes itself today: are the *new* orthotheses – constituted by analogue and digital technologies, but also those mechanical technologies that reproduce movement and that can be included in what Simondon called mechanology, technologies which have permitted the proletarianization of the producer and the consumer – do these technologies contain the potential to renew the individuation of the *I* and of the *we*, individuations that at present they undo, rather than supporting the possibility of their singularization, that is, of their affirmation?

In other words, what can be said *practically*, today – that is, in this epoch of the history of the supplement and of the grammatization that it supports insofar as it is a *system* of supplements – about this situation of wanting to believe that this epoch, for as much as it is possible, and each time that it is possible, accedes to another experience of singularity?

Generalized proletarianization concretizes itself through a dual exteriorization, formalization and standardization of *savoir-faire* and *savoir-vivre*. This generalized grammatization, that supports and concretizes generalized proletarianization, must also be that which supports and concretizes the possibility of a singularization – to the extent that the hypomnesic characters of machines and apparatus would become objects of culture, that is, of *practices*, and not merely of usages. But this could only be constituted as an industrial project of a political economy of the spirit of continental dimensions, as the organization of a system of supplements.

4. A plea for little rational accounts

Decomposition is not a fatality: it is a question of economy and of politics. Insofar as it inscribes itself in a struggle and aims at interpretations that are transformations of the world, the treatment of this question aims as well at prescriptions, which themselves presuppose systematic analyses of the singularity of the current epoch of grammatization.

The republican school was one such decision and a sustained repercussion of the second technological revolution of grammatization, that is, of printing, and was, moreover, preceded, as shown by François Furet and Jacques Ozouf,[19] by a religious literacy programme [*alphabétisation*], emerging in particular from the Reformation and Counter-Reformation: a literacy programme by clerics, either living in *otium* or engaged in worldly affairs, constituting in other words a limited education of the people, and to which corresponded a literacy itself 'limited'. With the philosophers of the Enlightenment, in particular with Condorcet, and with Turgot, the notion of the school as renewing the democratic or republican hearth was able to stimulate, on laic and political grounds, and at the very moment the industrial revolution was unleashed, the project of managing the access of the *demos* become 'people' to the *timiotata*. This was done through the systematic and compulsory development of the practice of *hypomnemata* across a form of public instruction instituting a new *otium* of the people, and which, as laic instruction, came to oppose the *otium* of the people that had until then dominated as the religious cult, and which, precisely, the philosophy of rigorous socialism (that communism was understood to be) went on to call the opium of the people. Furthermore, Ferry, after the founding work of Guizot, instituted an instrument of adoption corresponding to new needs, needs created, precisely in relation to adoption, by the industrial revolution: consumers as well as producers had to know how to control machines just as they had to be able to read the press that ensured the promotion of new products.

Now, we are today living the trailblazing arrival [*l'apparition fulgurante*] of a new age of *hypomnemata* that sweeps away the republican school, as the ideal of an *otium* of the people issuing from the Enlightenment and from nineteenth-century revolutionary struggles, and the political task in this regard is perfectly clear – and in this clarity it constitutes an absolute priority, just as school was a priority for the Church, and as it also was for revolutionaries: it is a matter of *struggling against this opium that certain media have, in effect, become* (whereas previously the press had been the condition of social struggle and of democratic and popular instruction, as Turgot claimed), in particular that media that aims to sell 'available human brain time'[20] to the producers of subsistence, but that, insofar as they are *hypomnemata*, can and must become practical supports constituting a new *otium* of the people. This is a state affair and, beyond this, an affair for public powers themselves profoundly rethought, given that it is also the nature of public space that here changes, and, in the first place, it is an affair for a European public power finally capable of replaying *the immense chance constituted by the accumulation of* hypomnemata, *in which its culture in all its hypomnesic and more generally its epiphylogenetic forms consists.*

But, reckoning with this situation, which concerns those new forms of *hypomnemata* that are the industrial mnemo-technologies, is a question of industrial politics as well as of spiritual politics: it is the question of a political economy of the spirit and of spiritual technologies in the sense of spiritual economy referred to by Valéry, and such that it is the sublimation of a libidinal economy.

And finally, this weighty task, that constitutes par excellence today's political responsibility, belongs firstly to those whom one calls 'intellectuals', whom I prefer to call thinkers, savants, artists, philosophers and other clerics (because, and I will return to this at the end, 'intellectuals' are, before anything else, *manual workers* and *technicians*, whatever it is they may think they are – and it is to this that they must henceforth give serious thought). In any case, it cannot be a matter of simply offloading this question on to those one today calls, with more or less contempt (more or less unjustified: contempt, when it is a matter of reflecting, is always an obstacle to thought), 'politicians', and, for example, of criticizing ministers and others, public and private, who are responsible for the future of the spirit and of its bodies and diverse incarnations – to do so would merely be to grant oneself a cheap alibi in order to avoid putting oneself to work, and would thus in the end be to discard one's own responsibilities. We must *surely* criticize the powers in place, public and private, economic and institutional, and so on, and, as well, academic and scientific, when they abandon their primordial vocation in order instead to integrate themselves, like clerics, into an apparatus leading to desingularization. But such a critique will in the future only be legitimate on the condition that we invent a field of discussions and propositions, leading towards practical questions, but also towards the *question of practices*, and towards decisions, towards *accounts*, whether petty or grand, in brief, towards *fictions*, but towards *good* fictions: *realizable* fictions, creating *movement*, designing motives, forging motivations – *accounts* that are in some way *rational*.

5. Fiction and the hand

Before continuing, I want here to make two clarifications, one about the question of decision, that is, about *political economy*, and the other about the hand. Let us begin with the latter, because it will take less time (but I will return to it at the end): grammatization is a *retreat of the hand*, and this is as such that in which the proletarianization of producers consists, contrary to the cliché that subsumes the proletariat to the working class, that is, to manual workers.

Nevertheless, this retreat of the hand understood as a retreat of the corporal organ of fabrication, to be replaced by the machine, does not only affect the producer: it is also that which makes the hand of the consumer become an ensemble of fingers that press buttons and lose their *savoir-vivre*, a *savoir-vivre* that supports the *savoir-faire* that their hands possess, as the right and left unities of the fingers. There is nothing disastrous about this retreat: it is a part of grammatization and thus it must be enacted. It is the continuation of what Leroi-Gourhan analysed as the retreat of the foot in the hand (a retreat of the motricity of the hand), and, again, I will return to this at the end. On the other hand, it has consequences that must be analysed in a detailed way: it forms part of the history of the supplement, which is as it were the description of the *becoming of organs*.[21]

The other, lengthier remark ties the hand to fiction, and fiction to decision. Grammatization is the pursuit of what Leroi-Gourhan and with him Jacques Derrida called (but with greater reserve on the part of Derrida) the *process of exteriorization*. This process is life insofar as it produces itself technically, that is, as *death*. It is death as that which *seizes hold of life*, but it is also life as that which *itself seizes hold of death*. Now, this seizing of life by death, and of death by life, is what appears in fiction, as the lure of fiction, whenever life is *opposed* to death, as occurs when metaphysics opposes and separates the immortal *soul* and the mortal *body*, and, in some way, the head, that is, *capital*, and *labour force*, which can become exhausted, and which we must therefore regularly *replace* – which means that, becoming merely a commodity, it becomes *replaceable in law as in fact*, which is what Marx denounces.

Be that as it may, however, *noetic* life is *intrinsically* fictive, fictional, and, as such, *to be decided*, decided *in the political economy* of this *libidinal and spiritual* economy that a city constitutes – it is deciding to *realize a fiction*. It is wanting to believe in a fiction: law, insofar as it is a difference we must *make*. Or to put it another way: it is to have *imagination* – or, yet again, *to invent*. Technics was suppressed as an object of thought *precisely* because it was declared structurally and irreducibly fictive. It is also for this reason that thought has been effaced from technics as fiction and from fiction as technics, to the profit of a thought of fiction *in language* and as opposed to truth in language, as *pseudos*, as lies and as moral questions – all on the basis of opposing essence and accident. If this operation is clearly something we find Plato engaging in – Plato, the great suppresser of the question of technics who, in some way, prevented technics from becoming the object of question, making it into something trivial – then twenty-five centuries of philosophy have consolidated this position and, today, the question of fiction, as essential to politics as it may be, has been profoundly *deformed by the metaphysical fiction* that turned it into a problem of morality and language.

My claim, however, is that this question is essential to politics, in the sense of being *definitional*: what is politics, in fact, if not the question imposing itself on human beings insofar as they live together, and insofar as living together, *they must make decisions, that is, create fictions?* Because *taking* decisions cannot be other than *creating* fictions, *transforming* the world – and making it in *conditions* of *tekhné*, that is, also, of potential, and of the *potential to access* dead or inherited *potentials* as pre-individual funds, which political beings arrange, or which they invent. On these decisions they do not agree, and they never will agree, *precisely* because these decisions rest on fictions, insofar as they *only are* [*le n'être que*] in being taken, and find their origin and their necessity in the (de)fault of origin, that is, in the felicitous incompletion of the psychic and collective individuation process.

Marx said the question was no longer to interpret the world but to transform it. Nietzsche specifies that all transformation of the world is an interpretation, and conversely. It is a question of generalized performativity, in the sense opened up by Derrida, but where this means a fundamental technicity of language, and where the question will *less and less* concern language, and will *more and more* concern the grammatizable *in general* – this generalization also constituting generalized proletarianization.

The city, having to make decisions, and therefore having to produce fictions that transform the world while interpreting it, seeks to find points of agreement: but *in metaphysics*, the agreement that is sought will be founded on *a* text that *would not be* a fiction, the transparent text of a foundational truth, a text that would not be, otherwise put, technical, or that would deny its own technicity, the text of the constitution of the good city, of the ideal city, which will rest on the exclusion of poets, precisely to the extent that the text is constituted (but also and in advance invalidated) by the denial of the constitutivity of technics – where technics itself constitutes a *power of fiction*. From that point onward, the fictive will be *opposed* to the true.

Now, today, after the industrial revolution and two centuries of machine-based capitalism, the question is to know how to *distinguish* good and bad fictions, rather than to purify truth of all fiction. But this passes through an entirely new consideration – an elevated consideration – of the question of technics.

6. Noesis as motricity and the reproduction of movement as the consistence as well as the irrationality of grammatization in the *being-only* [*le n'être que*]

As the analysis of temporal flows, in the first place linguistic flows, constituting their formalization, which is also their synchronization, their dis-idiomatization, in other words their de-diachronization, grammatization characterizes the history of this war of the Spirit conducted by spirits, a war that the conquering West has led for almost 3,000 years – and that led to capitalism. Yet while this process is clearly a domination machine, it also involves an intensification of singularities, but an intensification that is accomplished by displacements at the level of idiomatic differentiation. These displacements can be directly or indirectly translated into the terms of political organization. One major issue for this translation is the school, which, as I explained in *Technics and Time, 3: Cinematic Time and the Question of Malaise*, constitutes a political organization of selection criteria within the retentional systems that give structure to the pre-individual funds of psychosocial individuation, and that does so with a view to organizing the adoption of the pre-individual funds in which politics essentially consists, itself thought as a psychic and collective individuation process.

Now, with the appearance of the machine as the repetition of a process of transforming matter, a repetition in the sense that the machine becomes equivalent to a gesture, *grammatization becomes that of corporal motricity in general*. But we must here make clear that the grammatization of the word was *already* a grammatization of corporal motricity, but limited to the jaws, tongue and larynx, which together constitute the system of phonatory organs. This is, however, what metaphysics renders unthinkable. That grammatization takes on this motricity, that is, the motricity of the body, clearly has immense consequences for noesis, given that *noesis is before anything else the mode of the mobility of souls through their bodies* and in their relation to the prime mover.

Mechanization as a process of grammatization was very quickly extended to the new mnemo-technics constituted by analogical reproduction technologies in the nineteenth century, and by digital reproduction at the end of the twentieth century. This mnemotechnical grammatization continued the hypomnesic development of the West along an industrial path, so that the machine that reproduced the motricity of the body of the producer – that is, of the worker who had previously manually worked the world – continued to develop instruments of the *ars*, but in so doing disindividuated the worker who, losing his *savoir-faire*, and becoming pure labour-force – that is, a commodity – became thereby proletarianized. As for analogical and digital mnemo-technical grammatization, this enabled, on the one hand, the emergence of the figure of the consumer by massifying and reproducing behaviours no longer of production but of consumption, and, on the other hand, it enabled the functional and mechanical integration of production and consumption (this is what constitutes the hyperindustrial epoch of capitalism), resulting in a proletarianization of consumers themselves, progressively reducing existence solely to the conditions of pure subsistence, that is, to developmental imperatives conceived exclusively in terms of increasing the surpluses garnered from investment.

For all that, my belief remains that this becoming is self-destructive, or, to put it in the words of Jacques Derrida, auto-immune.[22] And this is my belief to the extent that I believe this becoming *destroyed the principle it was implementing to the precise extent that it was in fact implemented* – because the way in which this grammatization was implemented is hegemonically synchronizing, and excludes in principle all possibility for the intensification of singularities in which it could and must, on the contrary, *consist*. This self-destruction of capitalism relies in the end on that which constitutes itself as a libidinal economy, of which the principal motive has become the capture and harnessing of the libido of consumer-producers. This capturing and harnessing of libido can only be realized through a standardization of libidinal fluxes and flows, which is necessarily a *destruction* of these flows – to the precise extent that only singularity can put these flows *into move-*

ment, the movement of bodies and souls, their motive and their desire and, *as such*, their will. Through the very fact that hyper-industrial capitalism is a *total mobilization* of energies, that is, a form of totalitarianism, it destroys these energies and becomes the *impotent and immobile power* of a world within which reason is reduced to a *ratio* no longer able to produce any motive: it has become irrational.

7. Politics as struggle against the renunciation of *timiotata*

The industrial revolution, which was the beginning of these new stages of grammatization – stages which according to all evidence are ruptures in the history of the West, itself understood as grammatization – was at the same time the death of God, that is, the liquidation of a certain form of credit, and the appearance of new forms of credit, in the emergence, on the one hand, of capital insofar as it is credit, and, on the other hand, as the discourse of progress that came with it, a discourse that eventually came to oppose capital, but that did so by postulating another belief in progress, the belief in political emancipation through struggle: socialism.

Today, these forms of credit without belief have engendered a discredit that is a decomposition of the psychic and collective individuation process, a discredit concretely expressed in the production of generalized proletarianization, and such that, in the composition of synchronic and diachronic tendencies constituting both the singularity and the banality of an idiom – that is, the partition opening the *koine* in which it always already consists, the condition of all public space – the massification of consumer behaviour has led to the necessity of hyper-synchronizing conscious time, at the risk of completely de-singularizing individuation processes, and of thereby causing them to completely disband. Decadence is this disbanding. Nevertheless, this becoming is recent, and it was preceded by the development of capitalist credit conceived exclusively as calculation – which was made possible through an evolution of grammatization, notably in the sphere of accounting, that is, in the hypomnesic sphere of account-books, as Max Weber understood so well.

At present, grammatization opens the scene for decisions that must be taken, decisions that can only be settled through combat. Now, these combats are fictions: they are combats for a belief – that is, at the same time, for the *potential* of this belief, for a power which is that of hands or of that which ensues from them in grammatization, as technical manipulation.

I have in the second chapter of this work introduced the necessity of leading a combat that thinks itself in terms of the composition of tendencies, a composition within which that base [*vile*] tendency that wants to eliminate the duality of tendencies is always in play, whereas I have insisted on the inverse, namely that all individuation, as composition, is also always a combat, and first of all a combat against the renunciation of existence, a renunciation towards which all existence spontaneously tends, *culture being that which, at the heart of psycho-social individuation, organizes the struggle against this renunciation.* The renunciation of existence is a renunciation of becoming-other as future, that is, as *elevation.* It is what is produced between the intermittences that are these elevations, these *timiotata*, and that, forming the singularity of the psycho-social individual, describe the noetic soul that one more commonly calls man, for whom the fundamental movement is to rise up at the same time that he knows *before* all experience that he is inhabited by a lack or deficiency [*défaut*] in the form of weakness,[23] a weakness that drags him down, and drags him beneath everything that was conquered by his ancestors [*ascendants*]. At the beginning of the present chapter we saw with Aristotle that this base tendency is inscribed in the *psyche* just as is the potential for noesis, and that this fact is insurmountable: one must ceaselessly combat it. But, from the political point of view, this means that one must combat it *at the level of the organization of the process of psycho-social individuation.* This means much more than what Patrick Le Lay nevertheless explained so clearly, which was the way in which cultural and hyper-industrial capitalism exploits those libidinal fluxes and flows that are the fluxes and flows of consciousness, an exploitation consisting in very deliberately dragging noetic souls down to the level of sensitive souls: herding these souls and making them into human sheep, or even into human arthropods (which I described in 'The allegory of the ant-hill'[24]), that is, a planetary society of insects. The *timio-*

tata are that towards which it is matter of raising oneself, but this is only possible within the conditions offered by *hypomnemata*, and it is the role of organizations of political economy promising a future to make accessible and to support singular and individual (psychic) hypomnesic practices.

The history of the supplement thus henceforth requires a politics of the *hypomnemata* issuing from the three preceding industrial revolutions, themselves preceded by two technological revolutions of grammatization, the first being the epoch of the linearization of writing and of the appearance of orthography, which is also the epoch of the constitution of the *polis*, and the second being the epoch of printing and of what Sylvain Auroux calls 'linguistic tools', which in addition to being the epoch of the Reformation is that of colonization and of missionaries, that is, of the process of mondialatinization via the worldwide expansion of 'extended Latin grammar'.

8. The proliferation of *hypomnemata* and the noetic soul as the technical movement of the flesh

Action is always in some way a passage to the act of a potential, which means that action is always in some way *technical and as such practical*. And here it must be asked why practice has always been thought on the basis of the hand and as belonging to it. And this must be asked at the very moment when the hand withdraws in relation to grammatization – while *hypomnemata* proliferate.

The retreat of the hand is a chance and a trap. The trap is what I have described as the mechanical and digital integration of production and consumption, but where this includes the clerics and all the other old actors from the world of symbols, which is also the world of noesis in action, the world of *nous*, of spirit, of intellect, a world that finds itself integrated into the system of production through machines, what Lyotard called the age of the performativity of knowledge, and within which the 'intellectuals', as *manipulators* of symbols, become in their turn producers, but producers who, serving machines, or mechanical retentional systems, increasingly lose their *savoir-faire*, and, along with it, their theoretical knowledge, at the very same moment that consumers (which they also are) are losing their *savoir-vivre*.

As for the chance, it is that of rethinking noesis as *passing through* the hand. Because noesis, like grammatization, is technical, and technicity is first of all the technicity of the hand insofar as it *holds* that which made it originarily deficient [*fait originairement défaut*], and which it must be: a prosthesis, that crutch of understanding, reason and sensibility that are the *ars*, and of which I have tried to show that Kant's conception of the schema did not allow him to think, closing off any possibility for him to think technics, as can be seen in *Theory and Practice*, given that in this work technics is for him nothing more than applied science.

The grammatization process in which capitalism consists will eventually have the concrete outcome that the sphere of hypomnesis will be absorbed into the sphere of production, that is, the intellect will be absorbed into that sensitivity that is first of all, or at least reputed to be, that of the hand. And yet, we must also see this in an inverse way: it is the hand that would have been absorbed by the intellect, that will be held in the grip of the intellect – in the hands of the intellect, to put it figuratively . . . but this figure traces a vicious circle. It is in this situation that *hypomnemata* proliferate.

The nous *of the noetic soul is at bottom the technical movement of the body*, and the technicity of this movement is what describes the animation of this body, its *anima*, its soul – this body and that which exteriorizes itself of its soul through its movements and through the 'exteriorization' made possible by grammatization – at the risk of what Marx and Simondon describe as a loss of individuation. But we also know this was the very chance of singularity, or at least of that singularity that we want to preserve when we want to hold on to the possibility of political economy against an anti-political economism.

Now, if the will is a potential, or rather, the *act* of a potential, this potential is that of fictioning-in-action, that is, with the hands, *making* things with these hands, or with what has grammatized these hands in making them disappear – machines (which are never abstract, contrary to what is believed in very different ways but nevertheless jointly by Deleuze and cognitivism), including weapons [*armes*]: hands are also what one fights with, and these hands are sometimes bare and at other times armed, but it is always a matter of hands that fight because they manipulate a weapon, in potential or in act. And when the hands have disappeared, giving way to weapons [*armes*] without hands, it remains the case that these weapons affect bodies: the hand is after all a name for the flesh,[25] that is, for life, but precisely insofar as it is a deadly affair, and insofar as it makes death [*fait le mort*].

There would therefore be another thing that could be done [*chose à faire*] with bare or armed hands, or without hands: with machines. This thing consists in combat – within which one can make death or play dead [*faire le mort*].

Doing things [*faire des choses*], an expression that in popular language designates concupiscent behaviour, is always, in metaphysics, a villainous question, the question of villains, a vile question, in some way a question of hoodlums. Whoever says 'technics' says 'manual', and whoever says 'hand', in French at least, always also says, more or less, 'villain'. Hoodlums are thus often thought of as, and often in fact are, henchmen [*hommes de main*], men of the hand. Those who come with hands are those who are deficient in *logos*, insofar as this is the condition of the passage to the act of *nous*: they are not intellectuals.

And yet, if the soul is noetic to the extent that it is exclamatory, this is first of all because it has hands. That is, flesh: this body that it, precisely, animates. The noetic soul is exclamatory to the degree that it has hands, *of which the tongue* [*langue*] *would be only a case*, and whereby these hands are *constituted* through the process of exteriorization that is the concretization of this exclamation, a process within which, however, the hands themselves end up disappearing, and with them, the tongue in its mode of being manual. But this means that the question of the hand is that of technicity *beyond* the hand and which, through it, but *passing through it*, will be opposed to the intellect *like the evil to the good*.

Reading Jacques Derrida, along with Nietzsche (the genealogist), initiated me into what I here call composition – beyond what metaphysics constitutes as a play of oppositions. Composition *practically* consists in the thought that everything must be thought in terms of tendencies, which imposes thinking fiction as the *reducible* play of these tendencies: reducible to the fiction, *impossible in law* but *very possible in fact*, of *a sole* tendency, to the bad fiction of the *total* tendency, of *totalization*, of the suppression of *all* singularity.

Thought is a combat, but this combat must begin by thinking how and why the intellect has hands, which is also the fact of its *dunamis*, which is not simply its material, but its body, or its flesh, and such that it is constituted as flesh by the *fact* that these hands *hold* something – not to mention the fact that they can also clasp other hands, this last constituting an action which is, as Paul Celan said, sometimes like a poem.[26]

9. By default

We must [*Il faut*] preliminarily pose that *in law* (if not in fact) – because, as Jacques Derrida said, it is a matter of 'acceding' ['*faire droit*'] to singularity – one must not only *pose* but without doubt *impose*, that technics and singularity must be co-produced, that they can only be produced through one another. And one must oppose that which opposes this law – one must oppose all those facts that form obstacles to this law or, rather, one must oppose all that which, in the facts, *tends* to eliminate the possibility of this tendency that is *the right to singularity* – which is, without doubt, the condition of all those other rights that are clamorously demanded in the name of that overused expression, 'human rights'.

This is necessary, and it is necessary by default [*le faut par défaut*], that is: even without knowing how this is possible, or even *if it is* possible. Whether this is possible or impossible, one must affirm that this possibility is necessary. That technics can absorb singularity – and it is, as grammatization, an expropriation – is a possibility inscribed in the fact that it involves a *play of forces*, which is *also* the play of what Aristotle described as the *intermittence of the act within the permanence of potential*, which is also to say, seen inversely, the *permanent tendency to regression*. What I have described throughout this work as a process of decomposition of forces is the play of this regression such that capitalism toys with it at the risk of destroying itself. It is up to *us* [*nous*], and I say 'us' while I willingly admit that *I do not know* who this 'us' is, other than being those to whom is posed *in act*, that is, *in action*, the question taught to us here of *nous*, a question that is all the more open, generous and improbable given that I am ignorant about *who* this refers to while still believing, in advance and in principle, and in a fiction of principle,[27] that it is up to *us* to say that this tendency is self-destructive, and up to *us* to oppose it, to oppose it by affirming that this tendency is unjust, and that this fact does not permit any law, *has no* law, and tends to eliminate *all law*.

The question is therefore that of a combat that it is a matter of leading, and of a will that *poses* a state of law, that poses in principle the difference between law and the dominant state of fact, a state of fact imposed through forces themselves in combat – but in combat against singularity. This would thus be a combat against TF-1 – but, beyond this, all television, which is always either totally or partially financed by advertising, and this is what it is a matter of *changing*. This combat that it is a matter of leading, this response to the war being led against singularity, and which, if it is not engaged, will still and always allow the development of reactions coming from wounded singularities –

> what one calls 'petty nationalism', the nationalism of minorities, regional or provincial nationalism, and for religious fundamentalism, which often goes with it [and that also tries to reconstitute states], hence the '*regression*' which accompanies the acceleration of the technological process, which is always also a process of delocalization,

– this must be the constitution of a force, and a force that proposes. Now, such a force of proposition – and which must be imposed, as one says, through the force of its propositions, that is, of its ideas – must rest on an analysis of the current and future possibilities of the history of supplements as systems of supplements. Grammatization, as the pursuit of exteriorization, is thought, and must be thought as this retreat of the hand in which proletarianization consists, and that comes after the retreat of the foot that Leroi-Gourhan showed was the path enabling access to the 'gramme as such', that is, to a certain epoch of writing that corresponds to what I have here called the process of grammatization, such that it constitutes the characteristic orthotheses of the play of tertiary retention through which the Western psycho-social individuation process is constituted, and within which this tertiary retention is concretely expressed as *hypomnemata.*

I am here presuming that this Western psycho-social individuation process is finished and dead, but equally that this *catastrophe* opens the possibility of a doubly *epokhal* redoubling, that is, of another epoch and of a wholly other thought of that of which it would be an epoch. I have proposed that this possibility must integrate techno-logical individuation with psycho-social individuation, including in its becoming-hyper-diachronic structure, that is, in its *chronic instability*, as the obsolescence induced by permanent innovation. I have equally proposed that capitalism must become the support of this individuation.[28]

I add here that it is in the retreat of the hand that it is a matter of inscribing what must be made to happen, and that this 'must' [*il faut*] must be *the necessary (de)fault of the hand* [*le défaut qu'il faut de la main*], that is, the very fact that the *hand is lacking or deficient* [*fait défaut*]. But if the hand withdraws as an organ of doing, then it must DO *without the hand*; and this is only possible by rethinking anew what will have been the place of the hand in *logos* – that is, by rethinking practice, notably the practice of *hypomnemata.*

10.   Wanting to be [*vouloir*] and the power to be [*pouvoir*] one's wound: that is, one's defect [*défaut*], that is, one's desire – or, the supplementarity of the soul as susceptibility

The question of practice was scarcely at the heart of thinking when the idea of the republican school was developed. This idea belonged to an age for which grammatization was a way of accessing pre-individual funds. Its development depended on an enormous public investment that, alone, permitted the constitution of industrial democracies, which then flourished, and all of which have since become decadent. It is to the redefinition of modes of access to pre-individual funds – such that these modes would not be submitted to the imperatives of subsistence, but would be conceived *as the intensification of existence*, that is, of knowledge (it is a matter of *savoir vivre* and *savoir faire*) – that the entire political project of the future must devote itself as a priority. And this must be the project of a reborn [*renaissante*] Europe, and of a 'new belief' in Europe and within Europe, a project with which Nietzsche, who did not know America, was already occupied.

And here, the question is not of knowing *if* there is a chance for singularity, but of posing that what there is has a chance *only if* there is singularity. *There is* clearly a chance for singularity. It is *clearly* this chance. The question is that of *seizing* it: of *knowing* how to seize it, and how to *see* it, and how to *fashion* it in order for it to be seized, or to seize it through the fact of fashioning it and in order to make it visible – in brief, to *invent* it; it is a matter of seizing the chance, as improbable and indeterminate, unbelievable and yet believed, through the hand, as the prehensile organ that it remains, in particular to be able to lend itself and give itself the hand, or through that which will have succeeded it in the history of the supplement and as process of grammatization. This is what one calls a *political* question.

The question of singularity is not a 'supplementary' question, in the sense of the question of the soul as a supplement, but the question of the *supplementarity of the soul* as such, insofar as the soul is that which considers the *as such*, and which considers itself as such, as, in other words, the noetic soul. This is to say that one must think it not only in terms of a *logic* of the supplement, but in terms of the *historicity* of a supplement that makes objects, and that has always made the objects of combat. But the conduct of such combat presupposes an analysis and a critique of the state of supplementarity that is not, no more than is the law, a fact fallen from the sky, but is rather, today at least, a construction of capitalism, and, one could add, of capitalism understood as metaphysics, itself understood as the power of the head over the body and its spaces, territories, regions, and all that which, mortal, contingent, and accidental, has been *opposed*, since Plato, to the immortality of the soul, as the sensible is opposed to the intelligible.

Singularity is the heart of the socio-industrial machinery insofar as it constitutes the object of all libido, which, in its turn, constitutes *all* energy for production as it does *all* desire for 'consumption' ['*consommation*'], but also, to speak like Bataille, of *consummation*,[29] and especially, of that which *raises* and *erects* everything towards the plane of consistence. Now, this singularity of the object of desire is inscribed in an *organology* that demands study, and that shows that the bodily organs of desire never stop defunctionalizing and refunctionalizing themselves – in the function of becoming supplemental: from the sense of smell evoked time and again by Freud, to the foot that so interested the Greeks as well as Nietzsche, and to the hand that today withdraws itself.

As for this question of the retreat of the hand, like that of the foot but unlike the sense of smell, it is a question of motricity (even if the sense of smell was originally constituted as a sense of orientation and thus as an organ of motricity, if not a motor organ strictly speaking): movement is the meaning of the accidental, and this is what one must think through a general organology.[30]

If we cannot know *how* singularity can be produced, we do know that the psycho-social individuation process can only be pursued *as* the production of such singularity. Consequently, one must invent the future to be able to predict it, and it is less a matter of knowing *how* singularity *can* be produced than of producing it, in fact and in law, by inventing it: practising it, experimenting with it, and also prescribing it. Singularity, which is also called *idios*, is first of all a wound. It is a wound of the flesh that forms a defect [*qui se fait défaut*]. But one that is necessary.

Joë Bousquet was shot in the lower back on 27 May 1918, and he never again raised himself up: he finished his life bedridden. And yet he did, nevertheless, raise himself: that is, he became a writer, and he *wrote* his wound, and he wrote that he *wanted to be* his wound and that he had the *power to be* his wound – that is, his accident, his *event* (as Deleuze put it), but this means here his *defect* [*défaut*]:

> He apprehends the wound that he bears deep within his body in its eternal truth as a pure event. To the extent that events are actualized in us, they wait for us and invite us in. They signal us: 'My wound existed before me. I am born to incarnate it.' *It is a question of attaining this will that the event creates in us*; of becoming the quasi-cause of what is produced within us, the Operator; of producing surfaces and linings in which the event is reflected, finds itself again as incorporeal and manifests in us the neutral splendour which it possesses in itself in its impersonal and pre-individual nature, beyond the general and the particular, the collective and

the private. It is a question of becoming a citizen of the world. 'Everything was in order with the events of my life before I made them mine; to live them is to find myself tempted to become their equal, as if they had to get from me only that which they have that is best and most perfect.'[31]

This will – which for the writer and poet Joë Bousquet is that of a practice and power of writing, and first of all as power over oneself, but which is also the power of an impotence and of the impossible itself – this will is not that of the subject, of metaphysics and of mastery, but is rather a matter of being inhabited by the impersonality of a pre-individuality. It is a matter here of thinking according to another figure of the will, which would not be that of the plenitude of the subject, that is, of its originarity, but, on the contrary, of the subject's (de)fault of origin (and which requires that Stoic *quasi-causality* that constitutes the basis of the *Logic of Sense*[32]): the fact, precisely, that its origin causes its defect [*son origine lui fait défaut*], and it is the *necessity* of this defect *as* its origin, its source, its provenance, to which it must respond – and in which it must believe. My wound, to which I respond, to which I want to respond: I want my defects, I want to *be* my defects – that is, my idioms: my *shibboleth*.

11. The chicken and the egg

To combat is to strike a blow [*porter un coup*]. A blow is always a blow of the hand [*un coup de main*], and in French this is understood in two opposed ways [as an attack, but also as having the knack of something – trans.], two ways that I believe must be composed. Such would be a thought of the hand, or a thought with or by the hands, held by the hand, and as an archi-writing understood as an archi-hand or the flesh of all supplement, including and especially as the tongue [*langue*]: *even beyond the hand*; and what circulates around the circuit of desire are the *cries* that all this occasions in the form of exclamations, exclamations initially wielded by the hand as the representative of the whole body, including the tongue – the *slightest* gesture *already* exclaims. The hand is that which gives blows and, as strange as this may appear, that which, insofar as it is a part of the body from which it would not know how to separate itself, receives them in making them, eventually in sublime forms, and always in a *différance*. The *différance* of a violence. The hand having withdrawn remains nevertheless the flesh that desires to desire – and that calls forth the will that wants to want, and wants to be able to believe, and to be able to want to believe. But one must, then, before anything else and *without condition*, want to believe – like Jefferson deciding to sign, even if it means losing his head.[33]

Otherwise [*faute de quoi*, failing which], one would want to see the chicken in order to believe in the egg.

The egg is a fact.

It must be made.

At Speloncato, Haute-Corse, Rio de Janeiro and Paraty, Brazil, Épineuil-le-Fleuriel, Cher, pays du Grand Meaulnes, between the months of July and August 2004

Notes and References

Quotations (p. vi)

1 First paragraphs from Paul Valéry, 'Freedom of the Mind', *The Outlook for Intelligence* (Princeton, NJ: Princeton University Press, 1962), p. 186; final paragraph from Valéry, 'Our Destiny and Literature', ibid., p. 167.
2 Cited in Gilles Deleuze, *The Logic of Sense* (New York: Columbia University Press, 1990), p. 148.

Chapter 1   Decadence

1 Paul Valéry, 'Freedom of the Mind', *The Outlook for Intelligence*, p. 190.
2 Jacques Bénigne Bossuet, *Pensées détachées*, in *Oeuvres complètes*, vol. 2 (Besançon: Outhenin-Chalandre, 1836), p. 382.
3 When I speak of psychic and collective individuation, it is in the sense described by Gilbert Simondon in *L'Individuation psychique et collective* (Paris: Aubier, 2007), but to which I have added my own analyses, in particular in 'To Love, to Love Me, to Love Us: From September 11 to April 21', in *Acting Out* (Stanford, CA: Stanford University Press, 2009), and in *De la misère symbolique 1. L'époque hyperindustrielle* (Paris: Galilée, 2004), and which I am obliged to cite once again, for the reader unfamiliar with these works: 'I am not an *I* other than to the extent that I am part of a *we*. An *I* and a *we* are processes of individuation. As such, as

processes of individuation, the *I* and the *we* have a history. This is not merely to say that each *we* is a different history; it contains the additional sense that the conditions of the individuation of the *we*, throughout the course of human history, transform themselves' (*Acting Out*, p. 40). 'Simondon, in *L'Individuation psychique et collective*, shows that for the *I* to individuate itself, my individuation must participate in the process of collective individuation, that is, in the individuation of a *we* where, insofar as I am an *I*, I have always already found myself inscribed. *I* do not exist other than in a group: *my* individuation is the individuation of my *group* – with which nevertheless I am not confounded, and, moreover, I may belong to several groups, which may be in disharmony' (ibid., p. 66).

In *Le temps du cinéma* I have proposed that:

1. The *I*, as a *psychic individual*, can only be thought insofar as it belongs to a *we*, which is a *collective individual*: the *I* constitutes itself in adopting a collective history, which it inherits, and in which is recognized a plurality of *Is*.
2. This heritage is an adoption, in the sense that I can perfectly well, as the grandson of a German immigrant, recognize myself in a past which has not been that of my ancestors, and which I can nevertheless make mine; this process of adoption is thus structurally factical.
3. An *I* is essentially a *process* and not a state, and this process is an *in-dividuation* (it is the process of psychic individuation) insofar as it *tends* to become one, that is, *in-divisible*.
4. This tendency *never realizes itself*, because it encounters a *counter-tendency*, with which it forms a *metastable* equilibrium – and it is necessary here to underline that the Freudian theory of drives is singularly close to this conception of the dynamic of individuation, but so too is the thought of Empedocles, and of Nietzsche.
5. A *we* is equally such a process (it is the process of collective individuation), the individuation of an *I* being always inscribed in that of a *we*, but, inversely, the individuation of the *we* only accomplishes itself through these *Is* of which, polemically, it is composed.
6. What ties the *I* to the *we* in this individuation is a *pre-individual milieu*, which has positive conditions of effectivity, related to what I have called *retentional apparatuses*. These retentional apparatuses are supported by the technical milieu, which is the condition of the encounter between the *I* and the *we*: the individuation of *I* and of *we* is equally in a sense the individuation of a *technical system* (this is what Simondon, strangely, failed to see).

7. The technical system is an overarching system (*dispositif*) which plays a specific role (and into which each object is taken: a technical object only exists insofar as it can be *arranged* within such a system, and in relation to other technical objects – what Simondon calls the 'technical ensemble'): the gun and, more generally, the technical becoming with which it forms a system, are, for example, and according to Foucault, the possibility of constituting a disciplinary society.

8. The technical system is also that which supports the possibility of constituting retentional apparatuses, issuing from processes of grammatization, which deploys itself at the heart of the process of the individuation of the technical system. And these retentional apparatuses are what condition the arrangements between the individuation of the *I* and the individuation of the *we* in the one process of *psychic, collective, and technical* individuation (where *grammatization is a sub-system of the technical*), which then relates the *three branches*, each branch dividing itself into processual sub-ensembles (for example, the technical system, in individuating itself individually, also individuates its mnemo-technical or mnemo-technological systems). (*De la misère symbolique 1*, pp. 105–7)

4 Edmund Husserl, *The Crisis of European Sciences* (Evanston, IL: Northwestern University Press, 1970).

5 These discourses principally concern the law, global political organizations, the nature of relations and of international or transnational regulations, etc.

6 And that certain people therefore qualify with the term 'hypermodern', although in doing so the concepts of 'postmodernity' are thereby led into a trap, and for an essential reason, to which I will return in the next chapter, but which nevertheless does not completely invalidate Lyotard's analysis.

7 This ideology, which is not explicitly referred to in the law of competition, but which is nevertheless the underlying spirit of the Commission's 'directives', is a poorly digested form – an ideologization – of something that, within economics, and ever since Walras advanced the theory of general equilibrium, has remained controversial, even among the neo-Walrasians themselves.

8 Pierre Lévêque and Pierre Vidal-Naquet, *Cleisthenes the Athenian: An Essay on the Representation of Space and Time in Greek Political Thought from the End of the Sixth Century to the Death of Plato* (Atlantic Highlands, NJ: Humanities Press, 1996).

9 Stiegler, *Technics and Time, 2: Disorientation* (Stanford, CA: Stanford University Press, 2009).

10 E. R. Dodds, *The Greeks and the Irrational* (Berkeley, CA, and London: University of California Press, 1951), pp. 207–24.
11 Cited by Herbert I. Schiller in 'Vers un nouveau siècle d'impérialisme américain', *Le Monde diplomatique*, August 1998: 'Time Warner and Disney-ABC Capital Cities, two conglomerates whose turnover exceeds $20 billion each, producing film, television programs, books, magazines, discs, and extending their activities to the distribution channels for these products: cable networks, television networks, theme parks, etc. To have an idea of the sums in play, we can take the example of the *Star Wars* trilogy. Beyond the box office, which procured $1.3 billion dollars, the toys and the games brought in $1.2 billion; videocassettes, $500 million; CD-ROMS and video-games, $300 million; clothes and accessories, $300 million; and books and comic strips, $300 million more. This is in total $4 billion dollars in profit! In the same manner, some dozens of information giants (material and logical) immersed the American and global market with their products. Cultural production becomes an integral part of production in general, and the political economy of culture – of the workplace as of consumption – henceforth imposes itself as a crucial domain of research and analysis.'
12 The US Federal Communications Commission.
13 In fact, the recommendation of the FCC indicated to broadcasters that the objective was the year 2003, 2006 being the outer limit. This performative act has effectively and suddenly incited all the stations to re-equip themselves, thereby 'boosting' the American audiovisual digital economy, which is only just emerging.
14 Cf., Bertrand Gille, 'Introduction', *Histoire des techniques* (Paris: Gallimard, 1978), and my commentary in *Technics and Time, 1: The Fault of Epimetheus* (Stanford, CA: Stanford University Press, 1998), ch. 1.
15 Cf., Stiegler, ibid., and *Technics and Time, 2 : Disorientation*. Here I take the word 'epochal' in the sense of interruption and of putting in suspense, and of the opening of a new epoch. I have tried to show in *Technics and Time 1* and 2: (1) that technical becoming must be thought through the concept of the technical system; (2) that there is no human society which is not constituted by a technical system; (3) that a technical system is traversed by evolutionary tendencies which, when they concretely express themselves, induce a change of the technical system; (4) that such a change necessitates adjustments with the other systems constituting society; (5) that these adjustments constitute a suspension and a re-elaboration of the socio-ethnic programmes which form the unity of the social body;

(6) that this re-elaboration is a selection amongst possibilities, effected across retentional systems, themselves constituted by mnemo-techniques or mnemo-technologies, the becoming of which is tied to that of the technical system, and the appropriation of which permits the elaboration of selection criteria constituting a motive, that is, a characteristic reason and sense of an epoch of spirit, that is, a characteristic stage of psychic and collective individuation. On these points, cf., *Technics and Time, 1*, p. 231, *Technics and Time, 2*, pp. 60–2, and *Technics and Time, 3: Cinematic Time and the Question of Malaise* (Stanford, CA: Stanford University Press, 2011), pp. 6–7.

16 Originally published in 2003; translated into English as 'To Love, to Love Me, to Love Us: From September 11 to April 21', in *Acting Out*.

17 'To Love, to Love Me, to Love Us: From September 11 to April 21', in *Acting Out*.

18 Samuel Huntington, with motives which are certainly not mine, but which illustrate the extreme danger of the present time, writes that 'consumerism, not militarism is the threat to American strength'; cited by Jean-Claude Casanova and Pascal Gauchon in 'États-Unis. La puissance économique', *Encyclopedia Universalis* (originally from Samuel P. Huntington, 'The U.S. – Decline or Renewal?', *Foreign Affairs* 67/2 (winter 1988/89): 88).

19 And nothing would be more frightening than a biotechnological consumerist society. That is why it is not sufficient to condemn the obscurantism that opposes research in the sphere of the living. It is not only necessary to offer a critique of the technological becoming of biology, and, more generally, the technoscientific becoming of science, and of drawing consequences from this – more than that, in this sphere more than in any other, it is necessary to affirm the incompatibility of today's dominant consumerism with scientific developments in the sphere of life. It is thus that, today, the question of biopower is practically posed.

20 In the co-edition with *Le Monde*, 2–3 May 2004. (Actually, the article, by Alan Riding, was published in the *New York Times* on 26 April 2004.)

21 Care is, for both the Greeks and the Romans, that which constitutes the *excellence* of the beings which we are. This is the *Care* which, in a fable told by Herder, created *Homo* – a fable retold by Heidegger, in his existential analysis of *Sorgen*. Now, *Care* takes here (in this Roman mythology) the role of Epimetheus, and this is why it must be translated into Greek as *elpis*, that is, at once, hope, expectation,

and fear – in spite of the fact that Heidegger utterly neglected this point. I have developed these questions in *Technics and Time, 1.*

22 Similarly, basketball shoes (remembering that basketballers are those heroes of the American ghettos, then of the European suburbs) have become luxury items [*luxe dorées*], in some way Dior-ized [*diorisées*]. And I was once asked to participate in a strange debate, where men shod with such luxurious sneakers denounced the becoming-adolescent of the cinematic public and complained (despite being ensconced in their sneakers) of seeing in this the cause of the heralded disappearance of arthouse cinema – the head being ignorant here, as so often, of its feet, in spite of the important role of the feet (and of lameness) in the history of Western culture, as insisted by Nicole Loraux, and in spite of the famous statement by Leroi-Gourhan: 'everything begins with the feet'.

23 Through his project of a general mediology, Régis Debray opened the question of technologies of belief (or rather of what he calls, in wishing to establish distance, the 'make-believe'). I have myself developed this theme, firstly in 'Fidelity at the Limits of Deconstruction', in Tom Cohen (ed.), *Jacques Derrida and the Humanities* (Cambridge: Cambridge University Press, 2001). I have also written on the question of the make-believe and its relation to belief – which is not the same question, even if the two questions are inseparable – in 'La croyance de Régis Debray', *Le Débat 85* (1995). Behind these problems remains the immense stake of knowing how an analysis of belief can or cannot lead towards the rearticulation of political belief, because it is unimaginable that politics could be possible without belief – this, at least, is the thesis I defend. And I have explained in *De la misère symbolique 1* that an analysis of psychosocial individuation, which is the only framework within which an analysis of belief is possible, as well as an analysis of the technologies of the make-believe, could not be other than itself a pursuit of this individuation, and therefore a political affirmation, and therefore a political belief.

24 No more than any consistent and sincere statement – as Jacques Derrida shows in 'Faith and Knowledge', in Gil Anidjar (ed.), *Acts of Religion* (New York and London: Routledge, 2002).

25 IRCAM is at present working on the concept of a high-fidelity channel called 'sémantique', with many European partners, within the framework of the project, 'Semantic Hi fi'.

26 'The Emerging American Imperium', *Wall Street Journal*, August 1997, cited in Schiller, 'Towards a New Century of American Imperialism'.

27 On this point, as on other questions tackled here, cf., Stiegler, Nicolas Donin et al., *Les Révolutions industrielles de la musique* (Paris: Fayard, Cahiers de médiologie et IRCAM, November 2004).

28 Cf., *Les dossiers de l'audiovisuel* 80 (INA, August 1998). The obscurity of the European Union budget has prevented me from updating these figures.

29 'If Britain is to integrate with Europe – as I believe it should – media make better economic, commercial and social glue than a forced convergence of currencies' (Rupert Murdoch, *Papers and Documents*, Birmingham, 6–8 April 1998, p. 6).

30 Europe is a fiction: Europe does not *exist*. It was, is, and will be first of all a belief, the belief in its own self-consistence. And this is why the eternal question of knowing what Europe *is*, is not a good question. A better question is to know what Europe *becomes*. What exists is what has *traversed* Europe, to know how it was that the process of Western psychic and collective individuation became European and has today become global. And this process of European individuation will have *individuated an idea*, and an idea does not exist, has not existed, and will never exist – as I will show later in this work, an idea *consists*. Existence lies between subsistence and consistence, and only a consistence, as idea, can animate a process of individuation as that which becomes.

   When I say that the process of individuation originating in Europe has today become global, what I mean is that it has emancipated itself from its own continental territoriality. But this does not mean that it has unified itself; nor does it mean that European individuation is condemned to disappear. But it will continue to become only on the condition that it finds ways of intensifying its singularity through its participation in a process of individuation that has become planetary.

31 And, as such, as a cinema, as the Americans have so well understood.

32 And posed here is a genuine strategic question about the development of a European policy of free software. But this is only possible within a much more global policy in relation to cognitive technologies and cultural technologies, which together constitute what I call here the technologies of spirit.

33 Cf., on this subject, Jeremy Rifkin, *The Age of Access: How the Shift from Ownership to Access is Transforming Modern Life* (New York: Penguin Putnam, 2000).

34 André Leroi-Gourhan, *Gesture and Speech* (Cambridge, MA, and London: MIT Press, 1993), p. 360, translation modified.

35 Jeremy Rifkin, *The Age of Access*, pp. 157–8.
36 Leroi-Gourhan, *Gesture and Speech*, pp. 360–1.
37 On 15 July 2004, *Le Monde* published an article concerning a study
     by the IRI Institute that investigated a fall in the turnover of mass
     consumer products, an article which had for a title and subtitle:
     'Distribution is helpless in the face of "counter-consumers". For the
     first time in ten years, the sales of products of mass production have
     gone down, even though they have risen from 3–4 per cent per year
     for the last ten years. Among the reasons given is the rejection of
     mass consumption by a certain category of the population.' The
     joint director general of IRI speaks of "rupture".
38 In this regard, a quite recent declaration by Patrick Le Lay, president
     of the French TV channel TF-1, is of a confounding clarity. This
     was reported by *Le Monde*, on 11–12 July 2004, under the title:
     'Mr Le Lay: TF-1 sells "available brain time"'. 'Questioned, along
     with other chiefs, in a work entitled *Les Dirigeants face au change-
     ment* (éditions du Huitième Jour), the president of TF-1, Patrick Le
     Lay, noted that "there are many ways of speaking about television.
     But from a 'business' perspective, being realistic, the base, the job
     of TF-1, is to help Coca-Cola, for example, sell its product." And
     he went on: for "an advertisement to be perceived, it is necessary
     that the brain of the tele-spectator be available. Our programmes
     are there in order to make this available, that is, to divert it, and to
     relax it, to prepare it between two ads. What we sell to Coca-Cola
     is available brain time." "Nothing is more difficult," he continues,
     "than to obtain this availability."'
       In *Le Monde diplomatique*, 'The Time of Con-Games [*Le temps
     des attrape-nigauds*]' (August 2000), I wrote that 'what the pro-
     gramme industries sell are not programmes, but audiences for adver-
     tisements. The programmes only serve to attract consciousnesses to
     be sold. And in this market an hour of consciousness is not worth
     very much. Imagine a nationwide channel has an audience of 15
     million viewers between 7:50 and 8:50 p.m., and garners during this
     hour a net advertising revenue of 3 million francs. In that case the
     consciousness to which it addresses itself is worth 20 centimes per
     hour in the market for audiences.' I have attempted to theorize this
     becoming-commodity of the time of consciousness, which I call here
     the proletarianization of the consumer, from questions deriving from
     Kant and Husserl, in *Technics and Time, 3*, then in 'To Love, to
     Love Me, to Love Us,' as a process of *massification of conscious
     secondary retentions* so that it constitutes traces which organize and
     individuate the primordial narcissism of which the brain is, in effect,

the seat, as the organ of mnesic traces (and I will return to this later, in ch. 3, §6): this is what is here precisely formulated by the president of the leading French television channel. As for a deepening of the *relation between brain, retention, and protention* in general, and as for Freudian thinking in relation to this point, allow me to refer to the conference I addressed at the Tate Modern in London on 13 May 2004, under the title, 'Desire and Knowledge', at the invitation of Charlie Gere, available at: <http://www.arsindustrialis.org/desire-and-knowledge-dead-seize-living>.

These questions are at the heart of contemporary individuation, that is, also, at the heart of today's political and economic question. One must no longer leave political representatives and those with private and public responsibility in peace on this point. If genetically modified organisms and so many other environmental and alimentary questions are without doubt important, they are nevertheless minor when compared to these questions of mental environment and of legal and even legislatively favoured total brainwashing, where it is very clearly a matter of intoxication on an extremely large scale, leading to the planetary ruin of humanity and constituting a new form of totalitarianism. The responsibility of politicians today is before anything else to put limits on this totalization, but it is also the responsibility of each citizen to engage those politically responsible for this path, which will require much courage and resolve.

In other words, Patrick Le Lay, who pretends to support consumption, is in the process of destroying it (cf. ch. 1, n. 37), as mass distribution is in the process of destroying production.

39 A recent example is the affair of Marie L., who feigned, on 11 July 2004, a racist and anti-Semitic attack against herself and her baby. This terrible story calls for a long commentary, but that would presuppose greater knowledge of the case than I possess. Let's simply say that for me this incident is inscribed in a series: symbolic, psychological and political misery; fantasies surrounding the monotheisms with their real and terrible difficulties; but also social mimetism, that is, the herdishness and hastiness of politicians, who take advantage of the susceptibility of citizens-*cum*-consumers-of-politically-targeted-behaviour to having their emotions captured and harnessed, thereby treating them as audiences, audiences the 'attention' of which is sold by the mass media to every kind of advertiser, salesman or spin doctor. In this regard, the newspaper *Libération* published an analysis of the 11 July incident, as well as a clear and courageous editorial by Antoine

de Gaudemar, which was also a way of apologizing to its readers. In another, more serious register, of which it is however impossible not to think here, the *New York Times* recognized the errors it committed and the responsibility it bore for the way in which it had portrayed the situation between Iraq and the USA since the beginning of the crisis, which had by then become aconflict.

40   I speak of performativity, here, in the sense defined by John Austin: a statement is performative to the extent that the mere expression of the statement constitutes its enactment. The title of the work in which this theory of linguistic acts is formulated is: *How to Do Things with Words*.

Chapter 2   Belief and Politics

1   Michel Foucault, 'The Meshes of Power', in Jeremy W. Crampton and Stuart Elden, *Space, Knowledge and Power: Foucault and Geography* (Aldershot: Ashgate Press, 2007), p. 158.

2   Friedrich Nietzsche, *The Will to Power* (New York: Vintage, 1967), 'Preface', §2.

3   Nietzsche, *The Gay Science* (New York: Vintage, 1974), §377.

4   What I call grammatization is the process by which all the fluxes or flows [*flux*] through which symbolic (that is, also, existential) acts are linked, can be discretized, formalized and reproduced. The most well-known of these processes is the writing of language. It was Sylvain Auroux who forged the term 'grammatization' in order to describe this process:

> According to Sylvain Auroux, the alphabet constitutes a *process of grammatization* (a *becoming-letter* of the sound of speech [*la parole*]) which precedes all logic and all grammar, all science of language and all science in general, which is the *techno-logical condition* (in the sense that it is always already technical and logical) of all knowledge, and which begins with its exteriorization. The *third industrial revolution*, which consists in the spread of information technologies and the resulting redefinition of knowledge, belongs to this process of grammatization – and, more precisely, to the *third technological revolution of grammatization*, the second being, according to the definition of Sylvain Auroux, the print revolution [. . .].
>
> To grammatize means, according to Auroux, to discretize in order to isolate the gramme, that is, those constitutive and finitely numbered elements that together form a system.
>
> One must not confuse this [grammatization] with grammaticalization: grammatization precedes grammatical theory. [. . .] [T]he *technical* practice of grammatization, connected to various utilitarian concerns,

largely precedes these theories, which it conditions and makes possible. In brief, it is not the grammarians who invent grammatization, but rather grammatization, as an *essentially technical* fact, which produces grammarians [. . .].

In the history of the process of Western psychic and collective individuation, grammatization, as technical individuation, is a weapon for the *control of idioms*, and, through them, of spirit, that is, of retentional activities [. . .]. Auroux gives the example of the grammar of Ma, which according to Auroux was the first Chinese grammar, and which would later succeed in projecting Latin grammar into Chinese.

This grammatical projection of 'extended Latin grammar', as he called it, astonishingly close to what Jacques Derrida called mondialatinization, is what has permitted the West [. . .] to assure its domination of minds [*esprits*], *by controlling their symbols*, that is, *by imposing selection criteria upon them* in their own retentional systems. Grammatization is the production and discretization of structures (which weave together these pre-individual milieus and transindividual organizations and which support technical or mnemo-technical systems). (Stiegler, *De la misère symbolique 1*, pp. 111–14)

But it is just as true that the mechanical reproduction of a human gesture is a form of grammatization, just as is the algorithmic analysis of an image or a soundwave. The grammatization of gesture is what makes it possible to remove the existential dimension from it: it is in this way that it constitutes a loss of individuation, as Simondon described for the case of the worker who becomes the servant of the machine. This is also concretely expressed in the assembly lines of Henry Ford's factories and the Taylorian scientific organization of labour. Equally, the genetic analysis of life can be conceived as a discretization of the vital continuum related to a process of grammatization. It is in this sense that Jacques Derrida was able to inscribe 'grammatology' (a concept which precedes the concept of grammatization by twenty-six years) into the context of neo-Darwinism and molecular biology. The loss of individuation induced by the grammatization of the living would clearly merit very complex analyses. But this also concerns the fact that the relationship between agriculture and the process of vital individuation presupposes psychic and collective individuation, which Simondon analyses in *L'Individu et sa genèse physico-biologique* (Grenoble: Millon, 1995).

5 Ortho-graphy, that is, vocalic alphabetic writing, induces the textual process of *différantial* identification, that is, the identification of written statements paradoxically results in their interpretability, through a process of what Jacques Derrida has analysed as *différance*. On these questions, cf., *Technics and Time, 2*, ch. 1: 'The Orthographic Age'.

6 This is what Marx opposes to the infrastructure: the infrastructure is then the reality of the forces and processes of production that the superstructure entirely occludes in proceeding from it as a derivative phenomenon.

7 I return to this point in ch. 3, §6, p. 111, and I have developed these concepts of retention and protention on many occasions. A summary can be found in *Philosopher par accident* (Paris: Galilée, 2004).

8 Cf., Stiegler, *Technics and Time, 2*.

9 On this point, cf., pp. 10–13.

10 Eventually making way for what one calls the mathematics of trust, itself emerging from the theory of games. Jean-François Guyonnet and Gilles Le Cardinal have, for example, developed such formalisms at the Université de Compiègne.

11 Regarding *elpis*, cf., ch. 3, §2, p. 100, and §6, p. 179, n. 15.

12 And this other thing constitutes, as such, what I have called tertiary retention.

13 Friedrich Nietzsche, *Thus Spake Zarathustra* (Harmondsworth: Penguin, 1961), 'Of the Higher Man', §5, translation modified.

14 On this question, cf., the admirable analysis of Jean-Pierre Vernant, 'At Man's Table: Hesiod's Foundation Myth of Sacrifice', in Marcel Détienne and Jean Pievve Vernant, *The Cuisine of Sacrifice among the Greeks* (Chicago, IL, and London: University of Chicago Press, 1989).

15 Louis Aragon, *Il n'y a pas d'amour heureux*, in *La Diane française* (Paris: Seghers, 1946).

16 Gilles Deleuze, *Nietzsche and Philosophy* (New York: Columbia University Press, 1983), p. 20.

17 As elaboration of a super-ego.

18 Cf., Barbara Stiegler, *Nietzsche et la biologie* (Paris: PUF, 2000).

19 Nietzsche, *The Will to Power*, 'Preface', §2.

20 Jacques Derrida, in particular, brings to light in exemplary fashion the way in which metaphysics essentially consists in building oppositions which are in fact included within compositions 'older' than themselves.

21 Even if we must presuppose here that the appearance of a social organization which may be defined as the constitution of an 'ethnicity' – that is, of an *idiomatic* culture distinct from other cultures with which it exchanges – is a late stage of this process, which covers two or three million years.

22 This is the object of what I call, in *De la misère symbolique 1*, a general organology.

23 Certainly, this worker [*ouvrier*] only works to a limited extent: his works (*oeuvres*) are a matter of labour [*travail*] in the sense that they are dictated by need, by the necessity of the necessitous. Submitted to the yoke of *ponos*, the labourer [*travailleur*] only works [*ouvre*] the world – that is, inscribes his individuation – with his hands, in submitting to the conditions of the productive sphere, that is, in handling tools and instruments of work, isolated from those clerics who, free from these conditions, work [*oeuvrent*] and labour [*travaillent*] in the symbolic domain, mentally handling signs which don't appear to them as technics, but as forms and figures of spirit – even though the free activity of the spirit always passes through a manipulation of signs which alone makes possible mnemo-techniques, thereby establishing them as what I call tertiary retentions.

24 Max Weber, *The Protestant Ethic and the Spirit of Capitalism* (London: Unwin, 1930), p. 72.

25 'In agriculture, for instance [. . .] the interest of the employer in a speeding up of harvesting increases with the increase of the results and the intensity of the work. [. . .] However, [. . .] raising the piece-rates has often had the result that not more but less has been accomplished in the same time, because the worker reacted to the increase not by increasing but by decreasing the amount of his work. A man, for instance, who at the rate of 1 mark per acre mowed 2½ acres per day and earned 2½ marks, when the rate was raised to 1.25 marks per acre mowed, not 3 acres, as he might easily have done, thus earning 3.75 marks, but only 2 acres, so that he could still earn the 2½ marks to which he was accustomed. The opportunity of earning more was less attractive than that of working less' (ibid., pp. 59–60).

26 Ibid., p. 60.

27 Sylvain Auroux, who has insisted on the specificity of grammatization in the age of print, and on the politics of spirit implemented by Jesuits, by missionaries, and as an instrument of colonization, has not analysed the religious stakes at the heart of Christianity. On the other hand, this was the heart of the thesis elaborated by Elizabeth Eisenstein in *The Printing Press as an Agent of Change* (Cambridge: Cambridge University Press, 1980, new edn), a thesis later contested by Roger Chartier.

28 Cf., ch. 3, §4, pp. 106–7.

29 Benjamin Franklin, cited by Weber, *The Protestant Ethic and the Spirit of Capitalism*, pp. 48–9. Bataille shows just why this calculability of time is properly impious in the epoch of nobles and clerics: 'This would be to make time pay; and time, unlike space,

was said to be God's domain and not that of men' (Georges Bataille, *The Accursed Share, Volume 1: Consumption* (New York: Zone Books, 1991), p. 117).

30 'Nothing is more cynically opposed to the spirit of religious sacrifice, which continued, prior to the Reformation, to justify an immense unproductive consumption and the idleness of all those who had a free choice in life' (ibid., p. 126).

31 Benjamin Franklin, cited in Weber, *The Protestant Ethic and the Spirit of Capitalism*, p. 49.

32 Franklin, cited ibid.

33 Ibid., p. 51.

34 Ibid., p. 53.

35 Ibid.

36 Ibid., p. 62.

37 Ibid., p. 60.

38 Ibid., p. 61.

39 'Now the peculiar modern Western form of capitalism has been, at first sight, strongly influenced by the development of *technical* possibilities. Its rationality is today essentially dependent on the calculability of the most important technical factors. But this means fundamentally that it is dependent on the peculiarities of modern science, especially the natural sciences based on mathematics and exact and rational experiment' (ibid., p. 24).

40 Weber, ibid., pp. 67–8.

41 Ibid., p. 69.

42 Ibid., pp. 69–70.

43 Ibid., p. 70.

44 Ibid.

45 Ibid., p. 72.

46 Ibid.

47 Ibid., p. 74.

48 Ibid., p. 81.

49 Michel Foucault, 'Self Writing', *Ethics: Subjectivity and Truth* (London: Penguin, 1997), p. 207.

50 On this question, cf., Stiegler, *Acting Out* (Stanford, CA: Stanford University Press, 2009), pp. 15–16.

51 Foucault, 'Self Writing', p. 208.

52 This is the name I give for alphabetic writing, for reasons I explain in *Technics and Time, 2: Disorientation* (Stanford, CA: Stanford University Press, 2009).

53 This concept of tertiary retention receives further explanation in ch. 3, §6. Any artificial object can constitute an object of memory, and

I have called this process epiphylogenesis, thereby taking up the thesis that Leroi-Gourhan develops at the end of *Gesture and Speech*, where he proposes that technics is fundamentally the appearance of a third memory. Nevertheless, tertiary retention is not necessarily mnemo-technical. On the contrary, the appearance of mnemo-techniques induces a new retentional life, which is the beginning of grammatization, and of which the *hypomnemata* described by Foucault are cases.

54 Foucault, 'Self Writing', p. 209.

55 Ibid.

56 'How I Became a Philosopher', in *Acting Out*, as also in *Technics and Time, 2*.

57 Foucault, 'The Meshes of Power', p. 154.

58 Ibid., pp. 155–6.

59 Cf., ch. 2, §1, pp. 38–9.

60 On these questions, Gilles Deleuze maintains a very traditional and metaphysical conception, when, for example, he proposes that what he names 'the diagram' precedes the technological factuality that implements it, and even though he uses a word that immediately calls upon a form of grammatization. More generally, the beautiful analyses concerning the flux, the body, codes and territories in *Anti-Oedipus*, ch. 3, 'Wild, barbaric, civilized', nevertheless lack the question of hypomnesis and of mnemo-technologies, even though they are presented as an interpretation of the Nietzschean question of mnemo-technique. I will return to these questions in a work in progress.

61 Foucault, 'Self Writing', p. 207.

62 Foucault, *The Government of Self and Others* (Basingstoke: Palgrave Macmillan, 2010).

63 Foucault, 'The Meshes of Power', p. 158.

64 Ibid., p. 159

65 Ibid., p. 161.

66 Ibid.

67 Foucault, 'Self Writing', p. 209.

68 Ibid., pp. 210–11.

69 On *mélétè* as discipline of the self, cf., Stiegler, *Acting Out*, p. 20.

70 'In business circles, the new operative term is the "lifetime value" (LTV) of the customer, the theoretical measure of how much a human being is worth if every moment of his or her life were to be commodified in one form or another in the commercial sphere. In the new era, people purchase their very existence in small commercial segments' (Rifkin, *The Age of Access*, pp. 7–8).

71 Marc Crépon, *Nietzsche, l'art et la politique de l'avenir* (Paris: PUF, 2003).

72 Paul Claudel. I owe this citation to Pierre Sauvanet: 'Du rythmique, de l'esthétique au politique', at the colloquium *La lutte pour l'organisation du sensible*, Cerisy-la-Salle, 29 May 2004.

73 Cf., ch. 3, §6.

74 'Changing from the perspectives of *restricted* economy to those of *general* economy actually accomplishes a Copernican transformation: a reversal of thinking – and of ethics. If a part of wealth (subject to a rough estimate) is doomed to destruction or at least to unproductive use without any possible profit, it is logical, even *inescapable*, to surrender commodities without return. Henceforth, leaving aside pure and simple dissipation, analogous to the construction of the Pyramids, the possibility of pursuing growth is itself subordinated to giving: the industrial development of the entire world demands of Americans that they lucidly grasp the necessity, for an economy such as theirs, of having a margin of profitless operations. An immense industrial network cannot be managed in the same way that one changes a tire . . . It expresses a circuit of cosmic energy on which it depends, which it cannot limit, and whose laws it cannot ignore without consequences. Woe to those who, to the very end, insist on regulating the movement that exceeds them with the narrow mind of the mechanic who changes a tire' (Georges Bataille, *The Accursed Share, Volume 1: Consumption* (New York: Zone Books, 1991), pp. 25–6). We note that this text was written in 1949.

Chapter 3   The *Otium* of the People

1 Luc Boltanski and Ève Chiapello, *The New Spirit of Capitalism* (London and New York: Verso, 2005), pp. xliii, 8, 9 and 13.

2 Fernand Braudel, *Afterthoughts on Material Civilization and Capitalism* (Baltimore, MD, and London: Johns Hopkins University Press, 1977), p. 7.

3 On this point, cf., Stiegler, 'Allégorie de la fourmilière. La perte d'individuation à l'âge hyperindustriel', *De la misère symbolique 1*, as well as *Technics and Time, 2*, and *La Technique et le Temps 4* and *5*, both yet to appear.

4 Valéry, 'Freedom of the Mind', *The Outlook for Intelligence*, p. 190.

5 Valéry, 'Our Destiny and Literature', *The Outlook for Intelligence*, p. 167.

6   Jean-François Lyotard, *The Postmodern Condition: A Report on Knowledge* (Minneapolis, MN: University of Minnesota Press, 1984), p. 3.

7   'What is called capital is grounded in the principle that money is nothing other than time placed in reserve, available', Lyotard, 'Time Today', *The Inhuman* (Cambridge: Polity, 1991), p. 66.

8   Daniel Bensaïd, *Marx l'intempestif* (Paris: Fayard, 1995), p. 90.

9   Cf., ch. 2, §13, p. 87, and *De la misère symbolique 1*, pp. 20 and 129.

10 Sigmund Freud, 'Civilization and Its Discontents', in *The Standard Edition of the Complete Psychological Works*, vol. 21 (London: Hogarth Press, 1961), pp. 91–2.

11 Ibid., p. 115.

12 This is what I try to show in *Technics and Time, 3*.

13 Article 1, section 8 of the American Constitution: 'The Congress shall have Power [. . .] to promote the Progress of Science and useful Arts, by securing for limited Times to Authors and Inventors the exclusive Right to their respective Writings and Discoveries . . .'

14 'Producing' retentions therefore means, here, the same thing as when we say in French that a *judge* produces evidence.

15 And *epimetheia* presupposes *prometheia*, that is, the hypomnesic constitution of retentional possibilities (and anamnesic possibilities, but in the Proustian rather than Platonic sense) as a play of tertiary retentions. Cf., *Technics and Time, 1*.

16 Cf., ch. 3, n. 20. I will return to this theme in various works yet to appear.

17 Rare has become the politician who would not indulge in similar exercises, which induce the feeling of 'the shame of being human'. This fact must be placed at the heart of political thought, as the example of what must at any price be combated and denounced, as what we must oppose, and with which we must not compose. But who, amongst the 'intellectuals', accepting the 'passage to the tele', has not in some way sacrificed themselves to this nasty little game? Even Pierre Bourdieu delivers himself over to this at the very moment he believes himself to be denouncing it; I have tried to show why in *Technics and Time, 3*.

18 It is without doubt in order to distinguish the expenditure without reserve in which the sacrifice of consumption consists that Bataille forges the word *consumation*.

19 I have developed this point in a conference at the Tate Modern in London. Cf., ch. 1, n. 38. As for the question of the accident, I summarize this in *Philosopher par accident*.

20 And through which they metastabilize and configure what I call archi-retentions and archi-protentions. These constitute a pre-individual archi-fund which is the result of that which appears from Porphyry to constitute the question of universals: styles of pronouncements on archi-retentions and archi-protentions characterize onto-theological styles.

21 Hannah Arendt, *The Human Condition* (Chicago, IL, and London: University of Chicago Press, 1958), p. 7.

22 Ibid.

23 Ibid., p. 3.

24 Ibid., p. 9.

25 Ibid., p. 12.

26 Ibid., p. 14, n. 10.

27 Cf., ibid., pp. 15–16.

28 Ibid., p. 15.

29 Ibid., pp. 16–17.

Chapter 4   Wanting to Believe

1 Aristotle, *On the Soul*, 433a18–20.

2 Jacques Derrida, *Of Grammatology* (Baltimore, MD, and London: Johns Hopkins University Press, 1998, corrected edn), p. 84.

3 Gilles Deleuze, *The Logic of Sense* (New York: Columbia University Press, 1990), p. 148.

4 This text is a modified version of a speech that I delivered on 18 August 2004 at the Maison de France in Rio de Janeiro, at the invitation of Evando Nascimento, in the presence and in honour of Jacques Derrida, and in the framework of a colloquium which was dedicated to him, *Penser a deconstruçao, questoes de politica, ética e estética*, organized by the Universidade Federal De Juiz De Fora.

5 I adopt the Greek alphabet for this word, which is written in Roman characters as *nous*, so as to avoid confusion with the French first-person plural *nous*, of which we make great use in the problematic, which is here mine, as it is in many other of my works, of psychic and collective individuation, which is always constituted as the transductive relation between an *I* and a *we*, but also a *he*/*it* and sometimes a *He* (on this point, cf., *Acting Out*, pp. 66–71). It is, on the other hand, as fortuitous as it is striking that the French pronunciation of Greek *nous* is homonymous with the *nous* of individuation: is not spirit *precisely* that which, as *we*, that is, as *first-person plural without remainder*, cannot be inspected and appropriated by a people, a land, a tradition, a singularity, and

which, by this fact, can only be an *existing occurrence* of a *consist-ence* which is always for it *in excess* and, just as much, which finds itself thus *condemned to idiocy*, and, in some way, to the *clumsiness of idiom* which is never far from being stupid, and *stupidly regres-sive*, even though *it alone* can provide *by default* access to the spiritual *act*, to *this excess that is spirit* and to that which I will here call *noeticity* in action? On this subject, I think too of Kafka, of his relation to Yiddish and to German, and to the very beautiful paper that Marc Crépon dedicated to him, published as a book under the title *Langues sans demeure* (Paris: Galilée, 2005).

6 Cf., Stiegler, *De la misère symbolique, 1*.

7 Aristotle, *On the Soul*, 426b, where, apropos *to krinon*, Aristotle writes: 'It is not possible [. . .] to judge by the different senses that the sweet differs from the white. Rather it must be to some single thing that they are manifest. Otherwise from the mere fact that I see one thing and you see one thing it would be obvious that those things were not the same, whereas it can only be a single thing that asserts their difference. Sweetness, then, being a different thing from whiteness, it is the same single thing that asserts (*legei*) them to be so, and as it asserts so it both thinks (*noei*) and feels (*aisthanetai*) this.' (Translation slightly modified.) It is this concrescence, to take a word from Whitehead, of *legei*, *noei* and *aisthanetai*, that I des-ignate as *becoming-symbolic*, and that I characterize below as *excla-mation*. 'To feel' here translates *aisthesei*. But E. Barbotin wants to accredit the possibility of a common sense (the subtitle of the para-graph introduced by him to the table of contents is 'Common sense judges the senses and unifies knowledge'), which would be to make sense, as his translation introduces it here, equivalent to *krinon*, that is, to judgement, which he translates as 'judicative sense'. I propose, myself, to translate *aisthesei* as 'feeling' and *krinon* as 'discernment'. Because, in fact, what Aristotle says here is that a sense can only feel through comparisons, while making differences, *diapherei*, and in this it is as such *logical*, that is, logoic, taken in a *legein*, or in other words a gathering, where it is constrained to lose the singular-ity of the singular and to reduce it to the particularity of that which it enunciates, *legei*. And nevertheless, this does not mean in any way that there would be a 'common sense', which would necessarily be a sixth sense, since Aristotle expressly says elsewhere (424b22) that *there is not* a sixth sense. There is, on the contrary, a *community of senses* which enunciate themselves in *logos* and which is what makes the difference between the senses as singularities through being last, that is, in disappearing through the enunciation. It is thus

equally that the soul is only in action intermittently – and these intermittences are the passage of time, the fact that, in time, things only appear to the extent that they disappear, and to the extent that the significant becomes insignificant.

8   Martin Heidegger, *Plato's Sophist* (Bloomington and Indianapolis, IN: Indiana University Press, 1997), p. 92.

9   Aristotle, *Metaphysics* A, 982b31.

10   Cf., *Technics and Time 3*, chs 1–3.

11   This theme is reprised in *De la misère symbolique 2*.

12   Jacques Derrida and Bernard Stiegler, *Echographies of Television: Filmed Interviews* (Cambridge: Polity, 2002).

13   Ibid., pp. 80–1. My emphasis. Section in square brackets not included in French quotation.

14   My emphasis.

15   The phrase is, '*regard sur le monde actuel*', and the reference is to Paul Valéry's 1931 work, *Regards sur le monde actuel*, translated as *Reflections on the World Today* (London: Thames & Hudson, 1951).

16   The missions that converted the American Indians to Christianity, and which often prevented them from being massacred, came via the conquest of their minds [*esprits*], and it was a matter of unifying them in the Holy Spirit: this is what made possible the instruments (grammars and printed dictionaries) of the second technological revolution of grammatization, and opened the process of what Jacques Derrida called mondialatinization, what Sylvain Auroux studies as Extended Latin Grammar. In Brazil today, however, there lives, under the immense statue of Christ the Redeemer which dominates Rio at the height of 700 metres at Bao Vista, and which appears to watch over all of Latin America, *candomblé* and *macumba*, a fact which offends Pentecostalists and other Protestant sects deriving from North America, as Fernando and Chris Fragozo explained to me at the foot of this Christ the Redeemer – supported by the mountain like a Saint Christopher telluric.

17   My emphasis.

18   Cf., Stiegler, *La Technique et le Temps 4. Symboles et diaboles* (forthcoming).

19   François Furet and Jacques Ozouf, *Lire et écrire. L'alphabétisation de Français de Calvin à Jules Ferry* (Paris: Minuit, 1977).

20   Cf., ch. 1, n. 38.

21   This is what I today try to think in the sense of a general organology that constitutes, at the same time, a genealogy of the sensible. On these questions, cf., *De la misère symbolique 1* and *2*.

22 We must here underline that, as a process of adoption, and pursuit of grammatization, capitalism is a process of graft exposed to the entire question of the auto-immunitary reaction such as it was thoroughly explored by Jacques Derrida in his latter years.

23 This is what I will analyse in the final volume of *La Technique et le Temps*, as constituting a situation which I call 'atranscendental'.

24 In *De la misère symbolique 1*, p. 95.

25 I am certainly thinking here of everything that requires thought in Barbara Stiegler's work, *Nietzsche et la critique de la chair: Dionysos, Ariane, le Christ* (Paris: PUF, 2005).

26 Paul Celan, 'Letter to Hans Bender', in *Collected Prose* (Manchester: Carcanet Press, 1986), p. 26; cited by Marc Crépon in *Terreur et poésie* (Paris: Galilée, 2004), pp. 101–2: 'Only truthful hands write true poems. I cannot see any basic difference between a handshake and a poem.'

27 On the question of the fiction of principle that is a *we*, cf., Derrida, 'Declarations of Independence', in *Negotiations: Interventions and Interviews: 1971–2001* (Stanford, CA: Stanford University Press, 2002), pp. 49–50, where it a question of Jefferson's signature on the Declaration of Independence of the United States, and where Jefferson speaks at the same time in the name of the people that are nevertheless not constituted as a people other than through the signature of this declaration, and which, therefore, fictions this people in speaking in their name, but he is *able* and he *wants* (*il peut et il veut*) this fiction in which he therefore believes, and in which one sees the other face of this *God* in the name of which is proclaimed trust in the dollar.

28 Cf., ch. 1, §5, p. 17.

29 Bataille, *The Accursed Share, Volume 1*.

30 Such is the project of the collection of studies assembled in *De la misère symbolique 1* and *2*.

31 Deleuze, *Logic of Sense*, p. 148.

32 Ibid., pp. 142–7.

33 Derrida, 'Declarations of Independence', p. 48: 'You know what scrutiny and examination this letter, this literal Declaration in its first state, underwent, how long it remained and deferred, undelivered, in sufferance between all those representative instances, and with what suspense or suffering Jefferson paid for it. As if he had secretly dreamed of signing all alone.'

Index